T0366454

Ending Malnutrition

from commitment to action

Jomo Kwame Sundaram

Vikas Rawal

Michael T. Clark

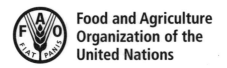

Food and Agriculture
Organization of the
United Nations

Tulika Books

Published by
Food and Agriculture Organization of the United Nations (FAO)
Viale delle Terme di Caracalla, 00153 Rome, Italy
in association with
Tulika Books
35 A/1 Shahpur Jat, New Delhi 110 049, India

©FAO, 2015

Cover design: Alpana Khare
Cover photo: ©M A Sriram/The Hindu

ISBN (FAO edition): 978-92-5-108872-2
ISBN (Tulika Books edition): 978-93-82381-64-8

Contents

Tables

Figures

Boxes

Preface

In November 2014, representatives from over 170 governments, together with leaders of intergovernmental organizations and civil society – including non-governmental organizations, researchers, the private sector, and consumer representatives – converged in Rome for the Second International Conference on Nutrition (ICN2). ICN2 was not a technical meeting; it was organized to mobilize and unite the international community for the protracted struggle against malnutrition. Organized by the Food and Agriculture Organization of the United Nations (FAO) and the World Health Organization (WHO), ICN2 and its preparatory process provided both a forum and event in which the world community, led by governments, affirmed its shared commitment to eradicating malnutrition by adopting the Rome Declaration, and reaching agreement on a comprehensive, harmonized Framework for Action.

A central contribution of ICN2 was to put sustainable access to healthy diets at the centre of food production, distribution, and consumption. The perspective was comprehensive. Through the Rome Declaration on Nutrition and the Framework for Action, countries committed to eradicate all forms of malnutrition worldwide: hunger or 'undernourishment' (inadequacy of dietary energy and protein intake); undernutrition (including micronutrient deficiencies, particularly during the 'first thousand days' from conception to age 2); and obesity and diet-related non-communicable diseases.

The Rome Declaration commits governments, *inter alia*, to ensure sustainable food systems for universal access to balanced and diversified diets. The Framework for Action sets out how to create an enabling environment for a wide variety of effective nutrition actions, including public policy interventions, to give effect to these commitments. The tools recommended are manifold: nutrition education and information; social protection to improve the nutritional status of schoolchildren, the poor, and vulnerable; scaled-up health system interventions to enhance nutrition; improved drinking water, sanitation, and hygiene; and enhanced food safety.

The 2013 edition of the annual FAO flagship report, *The State of Food and Agriculture*, took as its theme, food systems for better nutrition, and provided important background for ICN2. The report showed how various aspects of the food system – from inputs and production to transportation, processing, storage, retailing, food preparation, and consumption – influence the availability of diverse, nutritious foods, and affect people's access to and utilization of foods. Healthier, more sustainable food systems, the report showed, are key to securing healthy diets over the course of the life-cycle for all children, women, and men.

This book summarizes the role of food systems in improving nutrition, and highlights the measures necessary for its implementation on a global scale. It makes the case for more coordinated and concerted policy approaches, as well as greater international cooperation, to address malnu-trition in all its forms. It argues for increasing food availability through increased investments in agriculture, including by specifically promoting investments to enhance the availability of nutrient-rich foods. Such invest-ments are preconditions for a major breakthrough on nutrition, but, in many circumstances, the *availability* of more nutritious food by itself may not improve nutritional outcomes. By reviewing selected experiences of using social protection programmes to address hunger and malnutrition, this book argues for the expansion of coverage and the design of social protection programmes to ensure better popular *access* to adequate nutritious food – by ensuring both affordability and availability when needed. While recognizing the vital importance of appropriate fortification and supplementation in dealing with specific micronutrient deficiencies, the book cautions against placing nutrition supplements at the centre of the strategy. It argues instead for public regulation of and popular education about nutritional supplementation to prevent abuses and to ensure that profit does not take precedence over need.

In accord with the ICN2 consensus, the book also identifies comple-mentary actions required to improve nutrition. According to the latest statistics available, about 750 million persons in the world do not have access to safe water supply, while 2.5 billion people do not have access to improved sanitation. Closing these gaps requires political commitment at the highest level, involvement of all the relevant parts and levels of government, sustained fiscal support, and much greater popular awareness of health, nutrition, and hygiene.

The new post-2015 Sustainable Development Goals (SDGs), to be adopted by UN member-states in September 2015, present an extraordi-nary opportunity to invigorate the commitments and practical vision that emerged from ICN2. The ICN2 outcomes were formally welcomed in a resolution adopted by the UN General Assembly on 6 July 2015, with a decision made to consider other outstanding issues, including a follow-up programme of action, soon after the September 2015 UN Summit.

This publication is intended to provide a useful resource to policymakers, and their partners and supporters in civil society, expert communities, and the private sector, as they seek to transform ICN2 commitments and recommendations into concrete actions.

Vikas Rawal coordinated the preparation of the manuscript of this book. He is the lead author of chapters 1-5, and Michael Clark of chapter 6, on Governance.

Rome   JOMO KWAME SUNDARAM
1 September 2015   Coordinator for Economic and
                                                              Social Development
                                            Food and Agriculture Organization
                                                          of the United Nations

Acknowledgements

This book has emerged from the lengthy expert consultations and inter-governmental negotiations that led to the Second International Conference on Nutrition (ICN2) and the adoption of its two outcomes – the Rome Declaration and the Framework for Action – by consensus in November 2014. Jointly organized by the World Health Organization (WHO) and the Food and Agriculture Organization of the United Nations (FAO), ICN2 was a culminating event that drew on and contributed to growing global interest in nutrition. The ICN2 outcomes and their preparatory processes brought together a large number policymakers and experts from governments, academic and technical research institutes, international organizations, civil society, the private sector, foundations, and philanthropies. In so doing, it established a comprehensive new international foundation for collaboration.

The ICN2 preparatory process began several years before, with various consultations and materials on national circumstances and experiences commissioned and presented to expert groups to develop an evidence base for the conference. The FAO's flagship report, *The State of Food and Agriculture*, for 2013 focused on *Food Systems for Better Nutrition*, and helped to fill an important gap in nutrition policy by calling attention to the fundamental role of food systems in meeting – or not meeting – nutritional needs. It provided important guidance on steps to be taken to promote adoption of effective, evidence-based policies and regulation as well as informed consumers.

In this context, it is a pleasant but nonetheless challenging duty to record the many contributions that have been made to the preparation of this work. We must start by recognizing, *en masse*, the many colleagues who contributed to the ICN2 process, including the Preparatory Technical meeting in November 2013 and the complex intergovernmental negotiations, involving national representatives from both FAO and WHO, that produced the outcomes. The conference itself gathered more than 2,200 world leaders engaged in all aspects of nutrition work. Statements and declarations issued by individuals and groups at the plenary sessions, round tables, side events as well as at the four pre-conference events – the Scaling-Up Nutrition (SUN) Movement Global Gathering, as well as gatherings for parliamentarians, civil society and the private sector – further enriched the conference deliberations.

Some specific debts must be acknowledged. The entire ICN2 process could not have taken place without the crucial support of the Director-General of FAO, Jose Graziano da Silva, his counterpart Margaret Chan, Director-General of WHO, Oleg Chestnov, Jomo's WHO counterpart, as well as Fernanda Guerrieri, then FAO Directeur de Cabinet, and Coumba Sow from her office. Anna Lartey, FAO's Director of Nutrition, and Francesco Branca, her counterpart at WHO, have been patient, generous, and reliable guides through the demanding intellectual, technical, policy, and political journey to build global consensus on nutrition issues. Vital insight was offered at critical moments by Per Pinstrup-Anderson, David Nabarro, Flavio Valente, and others who helped set both the scope and tone for ICN2, and thereby influenced important judgments presented in this book. Virtually the entire FAO Nutrition Division, including Brian Thompson, Ali Mekouar, and Leslie Amoroso, made important contributions to the ICN2 process and outcomes, and thus to the views expressed herein. Dan Gustafson, Anna Lartey, and Dipa Sinha offered important comments, while Terri Raney, Andre Croppenstedt, and the SOFA editorial team who produced SOFA 2013 provided an important foundation for the perspective offered here.

The authors wish to express their thanks to FAO's Nutrition Division, and it's Director, Anna Lartey, for their strong support in all aspects of the preparation of this book. The production of this book benefited from the institutional support of FAO's Office of Corporate Communications, especially Jessica Mathewson, and the Society for Social and Economic Research in Delhi, and from the work of research assistants Mampi Bose, Bhawna Mangla, and Vaishali Bansal. Shad Naved's careful copy-editing of the manuscript is gratefully acknowledged. In addition, for all the statistical work and writing, the authors relied on R (www.r-project.org), org (www.orgmode.org), and LaTeX. All three are open source projects, freely made available by very vibrant communities of developers. During the course of the work, we often drew on support from these communities.

Finally, special thanks are owed to Tulika Books, and in particular, Indu Chandrasekhar, for approaching the publication in a spirit of true partnership that we hope will make the work accessible to a wider audience than would normally be the case.

While wishing to recognize the many sources of evidence and insight, criticism and encouragement that we have received in the preparation of this work, the authors take sole responsibility for the views expressed.

1

Uneven Progress in Reducing Hunger and Malnutrition

At the First International Conference on Nutrition in 1992, world leaders made clear in the World Declaration on Nutrition that, "Hunger and malnutrition are unacceptable in a world that has both the knowledge and resources to end this form of catastrophe." Over two decades later, the world continues to face several nutrition-related challenges.

In November 2014, the Food and Agriculture Organization of the United Nations (FAO) and the World Health Organization (WHO) co-organized the Second International Conference on Nutrition (ICN2), which brought together international organizations, national policy makers, practitioners and experts, to lay out a road map for coordinated action to ensure that no one in the world is left hungry and suffering from malnutrition.

How serious is the problem of malnutrition? Which regions face the various forms of malnutrition the most? Who are the most affected and vulnerable? What are the implications of malnutrition for the malnourished and for the world at large? What are the pros and cons of different policy instruments available to tackle malnutrition? What is the role of food systems in the strategy to end malnutrition? How useful are other means to provide nutrients? What are the means to improve absorption of nutrients?

These are some of the questions addressed in this book. It is argued here that ending malnutrition in all its forms – caloric undernourishment, micronutrient deficiencies, and diet-related non-communicable diseases often associated with obesity – requires a combination of appropriate interventions in food systems, public health, provision of safe water and sanitation, education, and social protection to guarantee the availability of and access to diverse diets; to reduce the susceptibility to disease; to improve the absorption of nutrients; and to increase consumer awareness of the importance of good nutrition. With widespread deprivation, unemployment, underemployment, growing inequalities as well as a slow and skewed economic recovery, a basic universal social protection floor will be crucial to guarantee access to nutritious food. While the use of nutritional supplements may be important in the short run, and in dealing with nutritional deficiencies faced by pregnant women and young children, in the medium and long term, a sustainable reduction in malnutrition requires a balanced diet. Access to safe water, improved sanitation, hygienic living conditions and basic health care are crucial for better retention and absorption of nutrients consumed by people. Sustained commitment to filling large gaps in these areas is imperative for dealing with malnutrition.

The ICN2 adopted two outcome documents: the Rome Declaration on Nutrition (Appendix A) and the ICN2 Framework for Action (Appendix B). The Rome Declaration on Nutrition, signed by representatives of over 170 countries that participated in the ICN2, gave a call for global action to end all forms of malnutrition. It identified focus areas for coordinated action. The ICN2 Framework for Action provides crucial policy guidance for governments to work towards meeting these objectives.

Hunger and malnutrition in the world today

The latest Food and Agriculture Organization estimate of the Prevalence of Undernourishment shows that, despite abundant food supplies and considerable progress in reducing hunger in some regions, more than 795 million people had chronically inadequate levels of dietary energy intake during 2014–16 (FAO, 2015).

"Hidden hunger", or micronutrient deficiencies, is much more widespread than hunger, which only refers to inadequate dietary energy intake. Although there is a paucity of regular and time-series data on micronutrient deficiencies, there is no doubt that the number of people who suffer one or more forms of micronutrient deficiency is staggering and much more than the number of people who chronically experience inadequate dietary energy.[1]

According to the latest data available from the World Health Organization's Vitamin and Mineral Nutrition Information System, about 1.6 billion people globally are anaemic.[2] Iron deficiency, the primary cause of anaemia, is only one micronutrient among many – vitamin A, zinc, and iodine, to name a few – missing from or insufficiently included in the diets of many around the world. According to data from the WHO's Global

---

[1] The problem of paucity of data on malnutrition is staggering. The recent *Global Nutrition Report* pointed out that more than half of the countries do not have data to assess the progress of six global nutrition targets accepted by the 2012 World Health Assembly (IFPRI, 2014).

[2] www.who.int/vmnis/database/anaemia/anaemia_status_summary/en/

Database on Iodine Deficiency, in 2003, about 2 billion people of all ages and about 285 million school-age children globally suffered from iodine deficiency (De Benoist *et al.*, 2004). Estimates for 1995–2005 show that 190 million pre-school children and 19.1 million pregnant women globally had vitamin A deficiency, while about 5.2 million pre-school children and 9.8 million pregnant women consequently suffered night blindness (WHO, 2009). Meanwhile, more than 1.5 billion people are overweight with half a billion obese, exposing them to greater risk of cardiovascular problems and other diet-related, non-communicable diseases.

Reducing caloric undernourishment

At the 1996 World Food Summit (WFS), heads of government and the world community committed to halving the *number* of hungry people in the world recorded in 1990 by 2015. Five years later, the Millennium Development Goals (MDGs) lowered the target to reducing the *proportion* of hungry people in the world by half. Considerable efforts have been made in many countries to reach these targets. Twenty-nine developing countries have made impressive progress, achieving the more ambitious WFS target, while 72 developing countries have achieved the MDG target of halving the proportion of hungry people (FAO, 2015).

Undernourishment is conventionally measured in terms of adequacy of energy in the diet. FAO's Prevalence of Undernourishment (PoU) is an internationally comparable, statistically validated, and widely accepted measure of the chronic inadequacy of dietary energy. Given serious data limitations, a methodologically consistent estimate of the prevalence of hunger can only be made for a relatively low benchmark of dietary energy requirement. The estimates of the number of hungry people in the world are also probably compromised by data and methodological limitations.[3]

Globally, the estimate of the proportion of people unable to consume minimum levels of dietary energy fell from 18.6 percent in 1990–92 to 10.9 percent in 2014–16. Over the same period, the proportion in developing countries fell from 23.3 percent to 12.9 percent (Table 1.1). While this is significant progress, it falls short – by 116 million persons – of meeting

---

[3] While the PoU is crucial for estimating hunger, it needs to be complemented by other measures to capture the complexity of food security in its multiple dimensions as this headline number for world hunger only tells part of the story of undernutrition. For this reason, FAO has developed a suite of indicators to measure different dimensions of food security, including availability, access to, stability, and utilization (nutrition). Information thus generated can shed light on specific problems to be addressed, and point the way to appropriate policy actions. FAO has also developed the Food Insecurity Experience Scale (FIES) as a tool to fill a crucial gap in global food security monitoring, particularly for assessing access to food at individual and household levels. The FIES directly measures the severity of food insecurity, defined as the extent of difficulty in obtaining food.

TABLE 1.1 Prevalence of undernourishment and number of undernourished persons, by region, 1990–92 and 2014–16

Region	Prevalence (percent)		Number (million)	
	1990–92	2014–16[a]	1990–92	2014–16[a]
Africa	27.6	20.0	181.7	232.5
North Africa[b]	<5	<5	6	4.3
Sub-Saharan Africa	33.2	23.2	175.7	220.0
Latin America and Caribbean	14.7	5.5	66.1	34.3
East Asia	23.2	9.6	295.4	145.1
South Asia	23.9	15.7	291.2	281.4
Southeast Asia	30.6	9.6	137.5	60.5
West Asia	6.4	8.4	8.2	18.9
Caucasus and Central Asia	14.1	7.0	9.6	5.8
Oceania	15.7	14.2	1	1.4
Developed regions	<5	<5	20.0	14.7
World	18.6	10.9	1010.6	794.6

Notes:
[a] Projections.
[b] Excluding Sudan, which became a part of North Africa after South Sudan became an independent country in 2011.
Source: FAO (2015).

the less ambitious MDG Target 1c of halving the share of chronically undernourished people. Unfortunately, the recent slowdown in progress is not encouraging (FAO, 2015).

The 2012 *State of Food Insecurity Report* provided additional measures of prevalence of inadequacy of dietary energy, using different benchmarks of minimum dietary energy requirement (FAO, 2012). The report showed that, in comparison with the methodologically most consistent PoU estimate of 14.9 percent in 2010–12, the estimate of the proportion of persons facing dietary inadequacy turned out to be 26.5 percent, if the dietary energy requirement benchmark was assumed to correspond to the minimum dietary energy needs associated with normal levels of physical activity. As per this indicator, referred to as Prevalence of Food Inadequacy (2), in 2010–12, 1.5 billion people globally faced dietary energy inadequacy.[4]

---

[4] Another indicator, Prevalence of Food Inadequacy(3), which uses a dietary energy requirement benchmark corresponding to minimum dietary energy needs associated with intense level of physical activity, showed an even higher number of persons, 2.6 billion, to be facing dietary inadequacy. For further details, see FAO (2012), Annex 2.

FIGURE 1.1 Prevalence of Undernourishment, by country, 2014–16

<5 percent
5-10 percent
10-20 percent
20-30 percent
30-40 percent
≥40 percent

Note: Map plotted using Gall-Peters projection.
Source: Based on data from FAO (2015).

FIGURE 1.2 Success in meeting the World Food Summit Target and the Millennium Development Goals Target 1c, by country, 2014–16

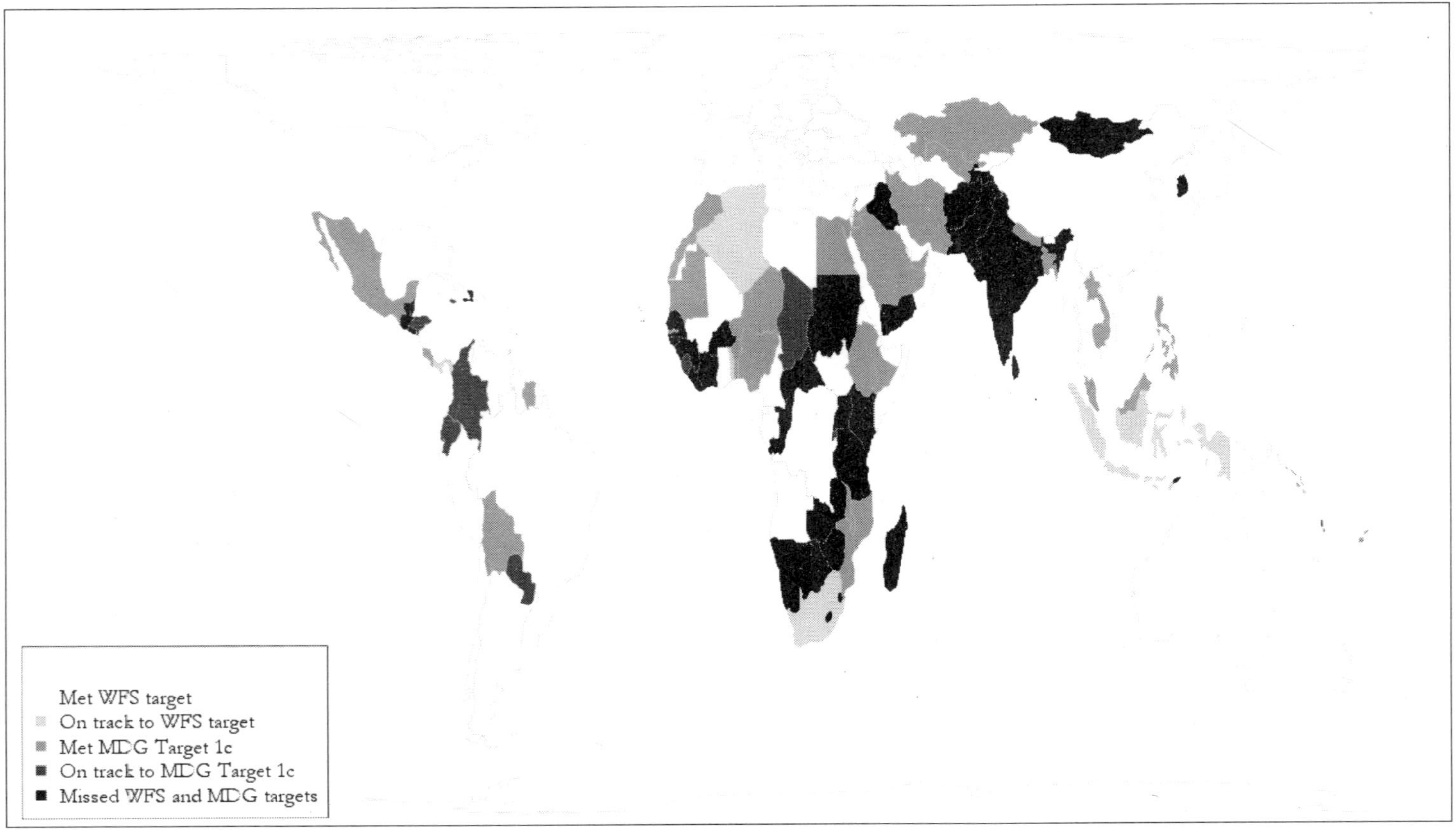

Met WFS target
On track to WFS target
Met MDG Target 1c
On track to MDG Target 1c
Missed WFS and MDG targets

Note: Map plotted using Gall-Peters projection.
Source: Based on data from FAO (2015).

Whether or not the MDG Target is achieved, the overall progress has been highly uneven. About 795 million people – one in ten people world-wide – remain chronically hungry even by the conservative definition used in estimating the Prevalence of Undernourishment. Of these, only about 14 million of the world's hungry live in developed countries. Some countries and regions have seen only modest progress in reducing hunger. In several countries, the number of hungry people has increased. Meanwhile, there have been significant reductions in the prevalence of undernourishment in most countries of Southeast Asia, Latin America, East Asia, Central Asia, and the Caribbean where the target of halving the hunger rate has been reached, or nearly reached (Table 1.1).

Progress in Sub-Saharan Africa has been limited, and the region has the highest prevalence of undernourishment by far, with almost one in four chronically hungry. Meanwhile, the more populous South Asia still has many more undernourished people. Progress in South Asia and Oceania has not been sufficient to meet the MDG hunger target by 2015, while West Asia and North Africa have had a rising Prevalence of Undernourishment (Table 1.1). Figure 1.1 shows the country-level variation in Prevalence of Undernourishment. Figure 1.2 shows that countries in South Asia and Sub-Saharan Africa have not been able to make it to the finishing line for the WFS and the MDG targets on hunger.

Slow and uneven progress in reducing malnutrition

Progress in reducing malnutrition has been slower and more uneven. Globally, about 15 percent of all children under 5 years of age continue to be underweight. Between 1990 and 2012, the number of underweight children aged less than 5 years declined by about 38 percent, from about 160 million to about 99 million, well short of the MDG Target 1c (Table 1.2).

In 2012, the World Health Assembly agreed to the following six global targets:

- Reduce by 40 percent the number of children under 5 who are stunted

- Achieve a 50 percent reduction in the rate of anaemia in women of reproductive age

- Achieve a 30 percent reduction in the rate of infants born with low birth weight

- Ensure that there is no increase in the rate of children who are overweight

- Increase to at least 50 percent the rate of exclusive breastfeeding in the first six months

TABLE 1.2 Estimated prevalence and number of children under 5 years of age affected by low weight-for-age, by region, 1990 and 2012

Region	Prevalence (percent)		Number (million)	
	1990	2012	1990	2012
North Africa	9.9	4.9	2	1
Sub-Saharan Africa	29.3	20.8	27	32
Latin America and Caribbean	7.3	2.8	4	1
East Asia	15.0	2.9	21	3
South Asia	50.4	29.9	86	52
Southeast Asia	31.4	16.2	18	9
West Asia	13.5	5.6	3	1
Oceania	18.4	18.8	0.4	0.2
Caucasus and Central Asia	11.6	4.5	1	0
Developed regions	1.1	1.6	1	1
World	24.9	15.1	160	99

Source: UNICEF, WHO, and World Bank joint child malnutrition estimates (available at data.worldbank.org/child-malnutrition).

- Reduce and maintain childhood wasting to less than 5 percent.

The recent *Global Nutrition Report* shows that at the current pace of change, the world is not on course to meet any of these targets (IFPRI, 2014). The report includes a detailed study of progress on four of these targets: targets related to stunting, wasting, overweight, and anaemia. Data on all the four indicators were available only for 99 countries. The report found that only one country of these (Colombia) was on course to meet all the four targets, and thirty-one countries were not on course to meet any of the four targets.

There are significant regional variations in malnutrition trends. East Asia has led all regions with a decline in the prevalence of underweight children to below 3 percent, followed by Central Asia, Latin America and the Caribbean, and West Asia. South Asia, with a 41 percent decline in the prevalence of underweight children, continues to be home to the largest number of underweight children. There were 52 million underweight pre-school children in South Asia in 2012. Despite a 29 percent increase in the proportion of underweight children, Sub-Saharan Africa had 5 million more underweight children in 2012 than in 1990 (Table 1.2).

A quarter of the children in the world, and a third in developing countries, are stunted due to a range of factors including poor diet. Four out of five stunted children live in just twenty countries, including almost half of Indian children under the age of 5. Although the prevalence of stunting fell from an estimated 40 percent in 1990 to about 25 percent in 2012, an estimated 162

TABLE 1.3 Estimated prevalence and number of children under 5 years of age affected by stunting (moderate or severe), by region, 1990 and 2012

Region	Prevalence (percent)		Number (million)	
	1990	2012	1990	2012
North Africa	29.2	19.7	5	3
Sub-Saharan Africa	47.2	38.0	44	58
Latin America and Caribbean	22.6	11.4	13	6
East Asia	36.7	7.9	52	7
South Asia	60	35.4	103	62
Southeast Asia	47.3	27.7	27	16
West Asia	29.9	18.1	6	4
Oceania	37.8	38.1	0.4	0.4
Caucasus and Central Asia	37.3	16.5	3	1
Developed countries	3.6	4.1	3	2
World	39.8	24.7	257	162

Source: UNICEF, WHO, and World Bank joint child malnutrition estimates (available at data.worldbank.org/child-malnutrition).

million children under 5 remain at risk of diminished cognitive and physical development associated with such chronic undernutrition (Table 1.3).

Nearly all regions of the world have experienced a decline in the number of children affected by stunting. The exception is Sub-Saharan Africa, where the number of stunted children increased by a third, from 44 million to 58 million, between 1990 and 2012 (Table 1.3). In Nigeria, over half of the poorest children are stunted, while children in poor rural counties in China are six times more likely to be stunted than urban children. In Indonesia, a sharp rise in wasting – or acute undernutrition – in the wake of the recent food crisis hit children from the poorest households hardest.

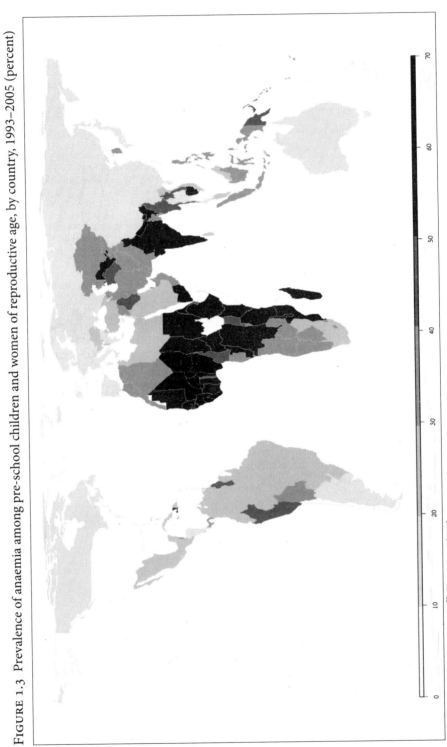

FIGURE 1.3 Prevalence of anaemia among pre-school children and women of reproductive age, by country, 1993–2005 (percent)

Note: Map plotted using Gall-Peters projection.
Source: Based on data from De Benoist *et al.* (2008).

FIGURE 1.4 Prevalence of iodine deficiency in population, by country, 1993–2006 (percent)

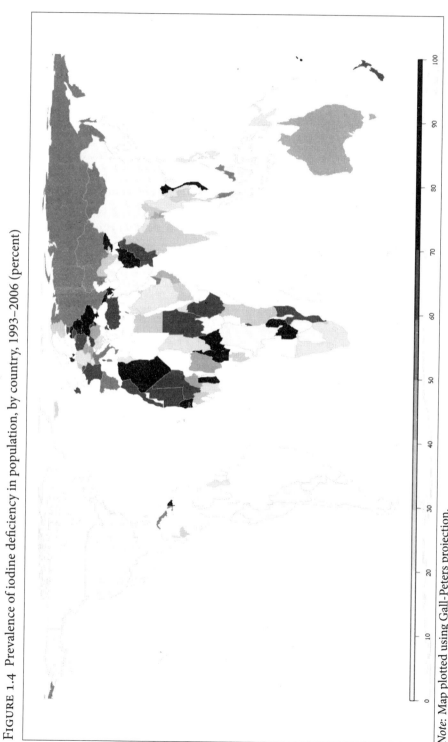

Note: Map plotted using Gall-Peters projection.
Source: Based on data from www.who.int/vmnis/database/iodine/iodine_data_status_summary/en/.

Consequences of malnutrition

Micronutrient deficiencies impair cognitive and physical development, especially among young children, making people less able to learn and work, as
well as more susceptible to disease and reduced life expectancy.[5] A detailed
review of studies and statistical evidence found that about 3.7 million
child deaths were associated with maternal or child underweight status.
These deaths and increased morbidity among children, from pneumonia,
diarrhoea and malaria associated with low weight-for-age, accounted for a
loss of about 127 million disability-adjusted life years (DALYs) (Ezzati *et
al.*, 2004). Horton (2008) estimated excess mortality globally attributable
to different types of malnutrition. She found 3.75 million deaths associated
with being underweight; 0.84 million deaths due to iron deficiency; 0.78
million deaths because of vitamin A deficiency; 0.79 million deaths because
of zinc deficiency; and 2.59 million deaths associated with being overweight.
Of the 8.75 million excess deaths on account of malnutrition, about 3 million
were in Sub-Saharan Africa, and 2.34 million in South and Southeast Asia
(Horton, 2008).

Studies have noted that receiving the right nutrients in the earliest years
of life is not only a matter of life and death, but also a major determinant
of future life chances. The evidence summarized by Ezzati *et al.* (2004)
shows that early child undernutrition is associated with impaired cognitive
development and lasting intellectual deficits. Undernutrition among adults
also results in diminished work capacity and lower productivity.

There have been some attempts at quantifying the economic consequences of malnutrition. Although such estimates have methodological
limitations, it is clear that the economic consequences of malnutrition,
particularly for the poorest and most vulnerable, are staggering. For
example, using data from ten developing countries, Horton and Ross (2003)
showed that the median value of per capita annual losses on account of
reduced productivity and reduced cognitive abilities due to iron deficiency
was about US$3.64 per year. For India, they estimated the value of losses on
account of reduced productivity and cognitive abilities to be around US$4.8
per capita per year. The estimated costs of malnutrition would be much
higher if the increased costs of health care due to malnutrition are taken into
account. The present discounted value of the lifetime costs of malnutrition
due to excess mortality, additional health-care costs, and loss of lifetime
productivity and cognitive abilities have been estimated to be more than
US$500 per capita (Alderman and Behrman, 2004; World Bank, 2006) and
US$2.8–3.5 trillion globally (FAO, 2013b).

---

[5] See Alderman and Behrman (2004) for a review of studies on the effect of malnutrition on
   productivity and cognitive abilities.

As rightly pointed out in the Rome Declaration on Nutrition, "malnutrition, in all its forms, including undernutrition, micronutrient deficiencies, overweight and obesity, not only affects people's health and well-being by impacting negatively on human physical and cognitive development, compromising the immune system, increasing susceptibility to communicable and noncommunicable diseases, restricting the attainment of human potential and reducing productivity, but also poses a high burden in the form of negative social and economic consequences to individuals, families, communities and States."

2

Transforming Food Systems to Provide Healthy Diets for All

Improving food systems is key to fostering more balanced, diversified, and healthier diets. As shown by FAO's 2013 report on *The State of Food and Agriculture*, food systems must be improved in ways that make such foods available and affordable (FAO, 2013b). Everyone should have access to a wide range of nutritious foods and be able to make healthy dietary choices. Consumers need help in making better informed dietary choices for improved nutrition with education, information, regulation, and other interventions. Improvements in post-harvest processing, storage, and marketing systems can reduce food losses and contribute to more sustainable resource use.

Regions and countries with the highest burden of micronutrient deficiencies also have a high prevalence of stunting and heavy disease burdens. The problems are closely connected and thus require a systemic approach involving all relevant sectors if we are to make progress. The food system involves people, institutions, agricultural production, processing, storage, retailing, transportation, commerce, international trade, and consumption. Improved nutrition involves and depends on every aspect of the food system. This is why an integrated approach is needed to ensure that food consumed is adequate, nutritious, wholesome, acceptable, safe, and affordable, especially to the poorest and the most vulnerable.

Creating sustainable and healthy food systems is key to overcoming hunger and malnutrition around the world. But food systems often do not function in ways most conducive to ensuring that everyone has access to safe food and nutritionally adequate diets. Improving food systems requires a systemic approach to deal with problems of food availability, food access, food safety, and of sustainability. We have to increase our efforts to address these problems.

Food availability

Globally, food production has more than tripled since 1961. The FAO's index of net food production, which measures changes in food production over time, increased from 34 in 1961 to 123 in 2013. Over this period, average food production per person increased by about 50 percent, with the index of per capita net food production increasing from 73 in 1961 to 123 in 2013 (Figure 2.1).

While the world produces enough food to feed everyone, there are deficits in food availability in various parts of the world. Inadequate production capacity at the national level, poor storage facilities and other infrastructure, and trade barriers still result in localized shortages in food availability.

In addition, political conflicts and natural disasters result in localized shortages. Protracted crises disrupt livelihoods. Natural disasters, conflicts and wars adversely affect agricultural production, trade, food access, social protection, and food aid (FAO, 2010). As an illustration, Box 2.1 briefly discusses the impact of the 2010–11 drought on food insecurity in countries in the Sahel and the Horn of Africa. Cereal production dropped 30 percent in Niger, 17 percent in Burkina Faso, and 11 percent in Chad as a result of the 2009–10 drought in the Sahel region. The 2010–11 drought in the Horn of Africa resulted in a 70 percent drop in cereal production in Somalia. Box 2.2 describes the impact of the Ebola epidemic on food security in affected countries of West Africa. The epidemic resulted in a shortfall in domestic production, reduced capacity for importing food, and

FIGURE 2.1 Index of net food production and net per capita food production, 1961–2012 (2004–06=100)

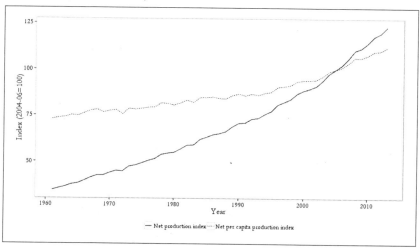

Source: Based on data from FAOSTAT.

Box 2.1 Droughts and Food Insecurity in the Sahel and Horn of Africa

The Sahel and the Horn of Africa are regions frequently hit by drought, poor harvests, and pasture deficits. About 20 million people are affected by food insecurity in the Sahel, and are likely to see their situation further deteriorate in 2015. Adversities on account of fragile ecological conditions have been compounded by conflicts in many countries in the region, which have resulted in large-scale displacement of people and disruption of livelihoods.

A Special Alert issued by the FAO Global Information and Early Warning System on Food and Agriculture (2010) described the conditions in Sahel thus:

> In 2009, agricultural production has been seriously affected in parts of the Sahel following late onset of rains, prolonged dry spells and significant pest infestations. The eastern and central parts of the Subregion were most affected with cereal outputs estimated to have declined by 30 percent in Niger, 17 percent in Burkina Faso and 11 percent in Chad, compared to 2008. Although favourable growing conditions boosted cereal output in most of the western part, irregular rains led to a 24 percent drop in cereal production in Mauritania.

> In addition to the decline in cereal production, pastures were seriously affected in the pastoral and agro-pastoral zones of Sahel. For instance, biomass production in pastoral areas of Niger in 2009 was estimated to be 62 percent below domestic requirements. This deficit is three times as severe as in the previous year. In Chad, a death rate of about 31 percent for cattle was reported in west–central areas, while in Mali, significant livestock deaths were reported in Timbuktu, Gao, Ségou and Kidal regions.

> Significant shortfall (over 30 percent in many areas) in Deyr rains (October–December) in 2010 and poor performance of Gu rains (April–June) in 2011 caused an extreme drought across the Horn of Africa, affecting over 13 million people. The impact of drought was further compounded by high food prices, very low levels of resilience on account of prolonged ecological stress, political conflicts and underdevelopment, and inadequate and delayed humanitarian assistance. In Somalia, the country that was worst affected, cereal production fell by about 70 percent. In pastoral areas, rainfall deficit significantly affected pasture growth, resulted in a decline in the availability of crop-residue fodder and production of livestock. Despite well-functioning early warning systems, conflicts in the region and consequent restrictions imposed on humanitarian assistance resulted in a famine that caused 260,000 deaths in southern and central Somalia alone. A detailed study commissioned by FAO's Food and Nutrition Security Analysis Unit for Somalia and USAID's Famine Early Warning System Network (FEWS NET) estimated that between October 2010 and April 2012, the period of famine, more than 133,000 children under 5 years of age died in southern and central Somalia on account of famine. The highest famine-related mortality was in the Lower Shabelle region, where famine resulted in death of 9 percent of the population and about 18 percent of all children aged less than 5 years. (Checchi and Robinson, 2013)

disruption of local markets, pushing about half a million people into severe food insecurity.

Disruption of rural livelihoods because of conflicts and disasters typically results in large-scale displacement and forces people to migrate, intensifying competition for scarce employment opportunities in non-agricultural activities, enhancing dependence on markets to obtain food, and increasing unsustainable exploitation of natural resources (FAO, 2010).

A more widespread problem on the supply side is the lack of adequate supply of different types of foods that should be part of a nutritionally adequate diet. Table 2.1 shows the average annual per capita supply of different types of food in different regions of the world. The table shows that Eastern and Southern Africa have the lowest average per capita supply

---

Box 2.2 Ebola Epidemic and Food Insecurity in West Africa

In 2014, the Ebola epidemic affected some of the most agriculturally advanced regions of Guinea, Liberia and Sierra Leone, with an adverse impact on agricultural production as well as household incomes from other activities. Trade restrictions in the face of the epidemic further contributed to problems of food availability as all three countries are net importers of food.

Reports from FAO and WFP suggest that restrictions on trade, hunting, and other economic activities have resulted in a large number of people experiencing severe levels of food insecurity. It was estimated that Ebola pushed 230,000 people in Guinea to severe food insecurity. In Liberia, 170,000 people were estimated to be severely food insecure because of the impact of Ebola. In Sierra Leone, the Ebola epidemic accounted for the severe food insecurity faced by 120,000 people.

The Ebola epidemic adversely affected domestic agricultural production in the three countries. The FAO–WFP assessment estimated that food crop production in Guinea in 2014 would be about 3 percent lower than in the previous year. In Liberia, the Ebola epidemic, which coincided with crop-growing and harvesting periods, resulted in an 8 percent drop in food crop production from the previous year. In Sierra Leone, aggregate food production was lower by about 5 percent. In the most fertile Kailahun district, rice production was estimated to be lower by about 17 percent.

Farms faced problems of labour shortages and market disruption as people feared the disease. With dysfunctional markets, transport and trade infrastructure within the affected countries, surplus producers were unable to sell their produce while consumers did not have access to food.

The Ebola epidemic affected not just domestic production in these countries. With international trade and border restrictions, export earnings fell sharply, resulting in considerably lower capacity of these countries to import food.

of fruits and vegetables. If we use the WHO norm of 400 grams of fruits and vegetable consumption per capita per day, all of Africa (except the north), South Asia, Southeast Asia, and Central America do not even have supplies of fruits and vegetables to meet that level of consumption. Fruits and vegetables are often seasonally produced and highly perishable. It is estimated that, globally, about 17 percent of fruits and vegetables are lost between farm and plate.[1] If one takes into account losses and waste, there would be considerable shortfalls in the availability of fruits and vegetables in most parts of the world.

Several factors constrain the supply of fruits and vegetables. The high costs and riskiness of production, poor access to credit, poor coverage and quality of extension services, and labour shortages during periods of peak labour requirement are among the factors that constrain the expansion of production of fruits and vegetables. On the other hand, limited shelf-life, poor packaging, storage and transportation, as well as price volatility and seasonality constrain the supply and marketing of fruits and vegetables.[2]

Recommended levels of intake for most other types of foods, as specified in Food-based Dietary Guidelines of different countries, vary across countries and with population groups. It is nevertheless useful to have an overview of variations in the supply of different types of food across regions and countries. There are wide variations – from very little to very high levels of supply driven by excessive consumption – in the supply of animal-source foods across different regions of the world. In 2011, Europe, Oceania and North America had milk supplies of over 200 kilograms per capita per year, while it was only 48 kilograms of milk per capita per year in Africa, and 58 kilograms per capita per year in Asia. In the case of meats and offals, Oceania and North America had a per capita supply of over 100 kilograms per year, while it was only 20 kilograms per capita per year in Africa, 33 kilograms per capita per year in Asia, and 44 kilograms per capita per year in the world as a whole (Table 2.1).

As seen in Figures 2.2–2.4, there are considerable variations in the supply of different types of food across countries within each region.

---

[1] In addition, about 20 percent of fruits and vegetables are lost during the process of harvesting, picking, and sorting, and therefore do not even enter the supply chain. Also, about 19 percent of fruits and vegetables globally are wasted by retailers and consumers because of poor storage and excessive servings (FAO, 2011a).

[2] See Ali and Tsou (1997) for an overview of factors that constrain the supply of fruits and vegetables.

TABLE 2.1 Supply of different types of foods, by regions of the world, 2011 (kilogram per capita per year)

Region	Cereals and pulses	Starchy roots and tubers	Fruits and vegetables	Milk (excluding butter)	Eggs	Meats and offals	Aquatic products
East Africa	136	120	79	44	1	13	5
Middle Africa	119	186	138	16	1	26	15
North Africa	223	38	244	106	4	29	13
South Africa	180	40	82	55	7	60	6
West Africa	152	211	114	20	2	14	16
Africa	161	131	130	48	2	20	11
Central Asia	163	68	265	169	6	46	2
East Asia	149	63	385	34	18	60	44
South Asia	169	33	127	83	2	8	7
Southeast Asia	172	39	132	18	6	31	33
West Asia	187	33	238	110	6	38	7
Asia	163	46	234	58	9	33	25
Europe	134	84	210	219	13	79	22
Oceania	94	62	185	203	7	123	27
North America	109	62	214	253	14	116	22
Central America	161	16	144	104	15	58	9
Caribbean	122	68	216	65	6	48	9
South America	127	66	170	140	9	32	10
Americas	126	56	183	173	12	39	14
World	154	64	210	90	9	44	21

Source: Based on data from FAOSTAT.

FIGURE 2.2 Per capita availability of cereals, by country, 2011 (kcal per capita per day)

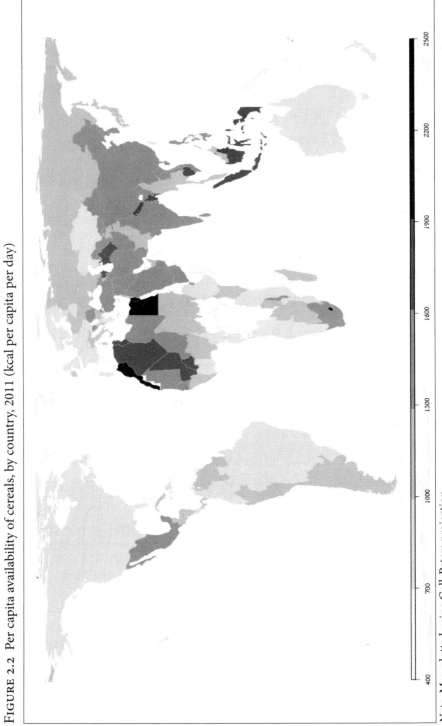

Note: Map plotted using Gall-Peters projection.
Source: Based on data from FAOSTAT.

FIGURE 2.3 Per capita availability of fruits and vegetables, by country, 2011 (kcal per capita per day)

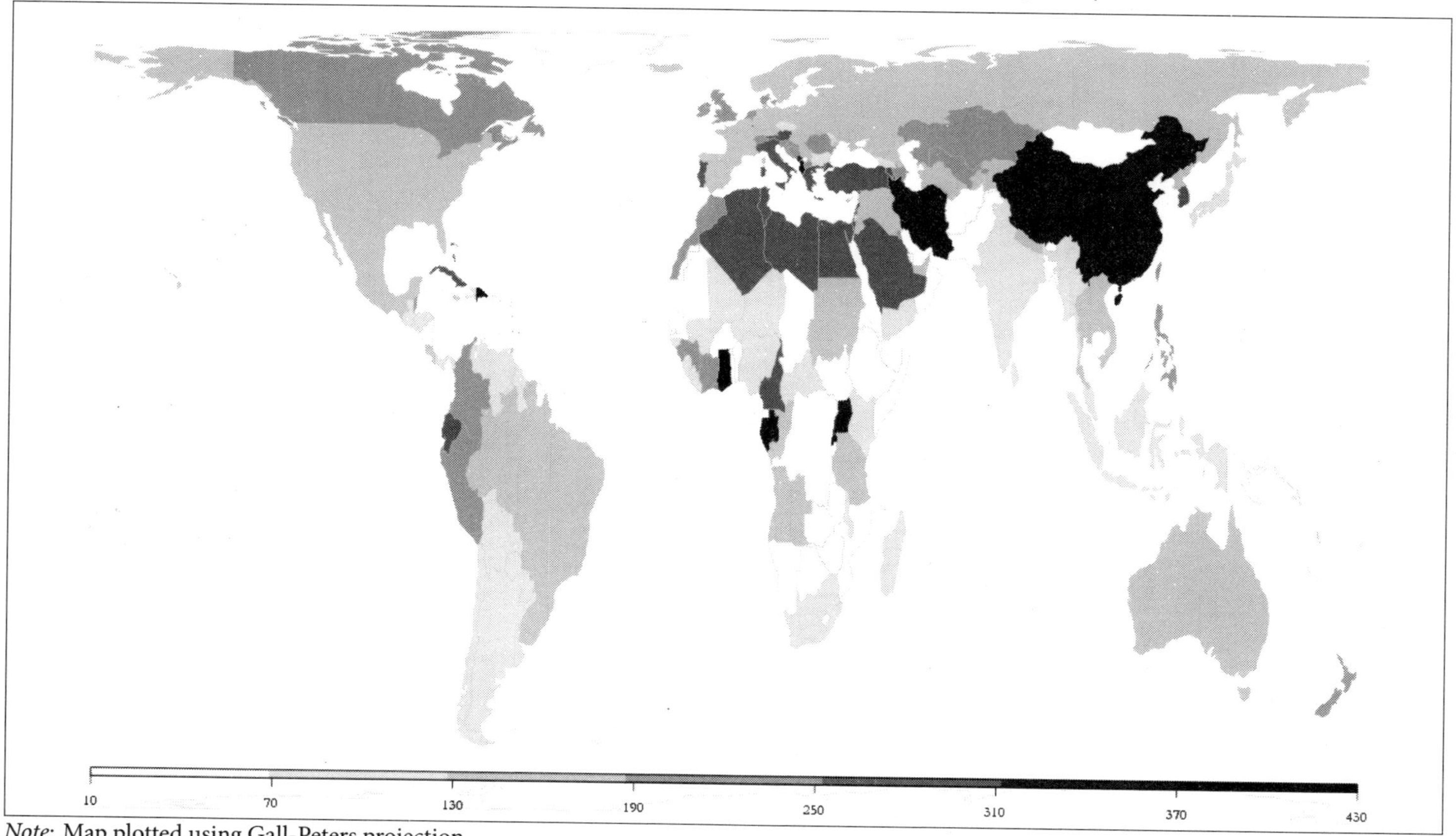

Note: Map plotted using Gall-Peters projection.
Source: Based on data from FAOSTAT.

FIGURE 2.4 Per capita availability of food from animal sources, by country, 2011 (kcal per capita per day)

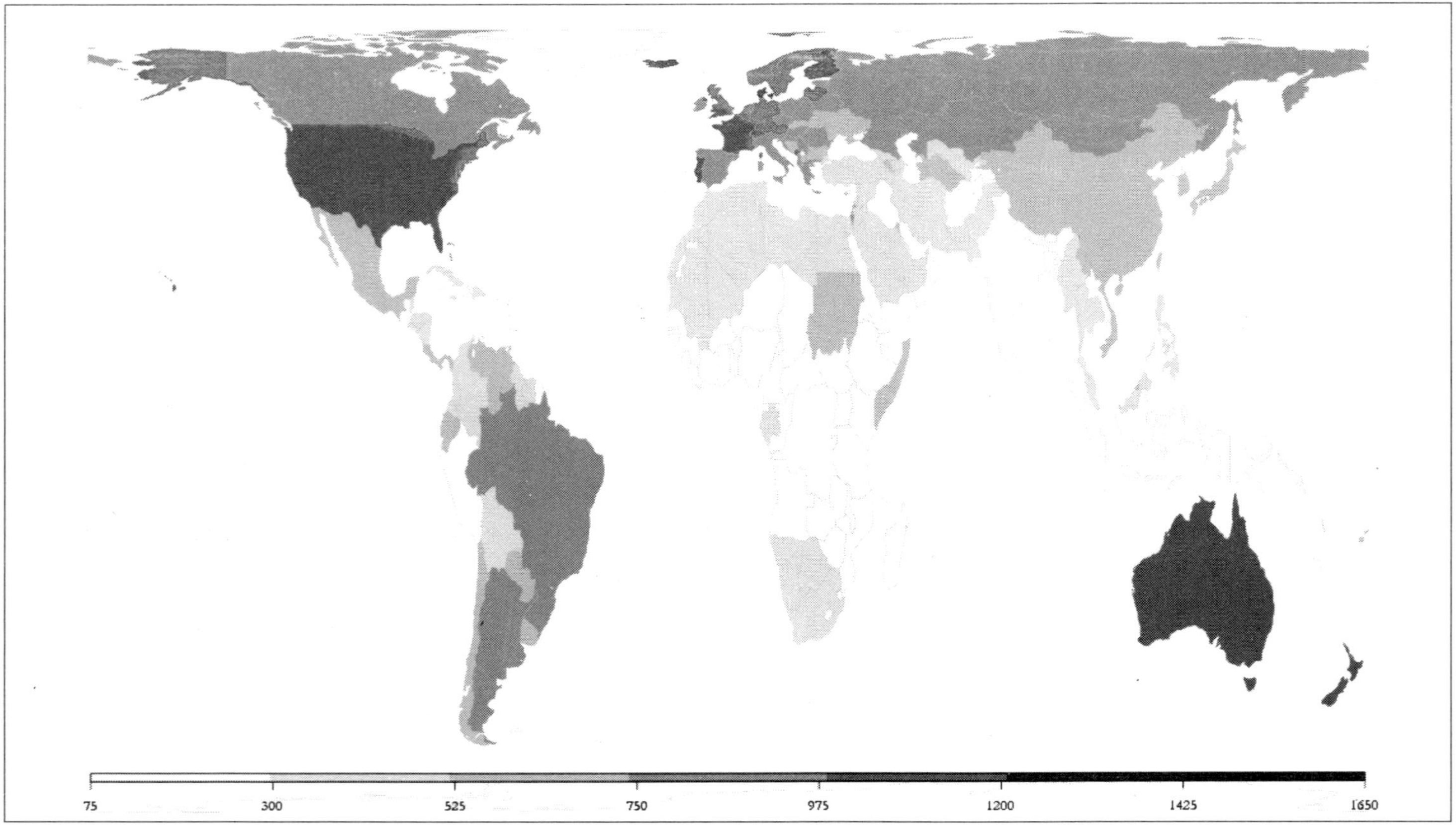

Note: Map plotted using Gall-Peters projection.
Source: Based on data from FAOSTAT.

75   300   525   750   975   1200   1425   1650

Access to adequate and nutritious food

Access to food is a critical dimension of food security. Having access to food requires that people have command over adequate resources to be able to acquire – through own-production, purchase or public provision – adequate and nutritious food. This brings into focus issues like access to land and other productive resources, household incomes and food prices. In addition, there is also the issue of physical access to food, particularly for people living in remote areas that do not have good transport and storage infrastructure, and for perishable food items, which lose their nutritional value and wholesomeness quickly under poor storage conditions.

Food prices and access to food

The world saw sharp rises in global food prices in 2007–08 and 2010–11. These price spikes were fuelled, most importantly, by a mandated increase in the use of food crops for biofuels, resulting in increased integration of food and oil prices, and increased speculation in commodity prices. Systematic reviews of evidence from across the world show that the food price spikes of 2007–08 and 2010–11 adversely affected the food security of the world's poor (FAO, 2008, 2011b; HLPE, 2011). Although high food prices, if transmitted to producers, benefit surplus producers, the vast proportion of the urban and rural poor are net buyers of food, and are adversely hit by rising food prices. The high volatility of food prices creates considerable uncertainty in the food system and discourages long-term investment (FAO, 2011b; HLPE, 2011). High food prices particularly hit poor buyers of food who spend large shares of their incomes on food. Empirical evidence also shows that rising global food prices in 2007–08 and 2010–11 adversely affected dietary diversity, as the poor shifted to the most inexpensive and nutrient-poor food items to meet their dietary energy requirements. Such dietary changes have increased micronutrient deficiencies and exacerbated malnutrition among children (HLPE, 2011).

With the easing of global food prices, there has been some decline in the proportion of undernourished people globally. However, according to the latest Prevalence of Undernourishment estimates (Table 1.1), about 800 million people still do not get to consume enough food to meet even their minimum dietary energy requirements.

Access and diet quality

Surveys of consumption and diet quality show considerable inequality, not only in overall levels of food consumption, but also in diet quality across economic classes and among different populations in different countries.

Darmon and Drewnowski (2008) have done a detailed review of the literature on the relationship of socio-economic status with diet quality,

Box 2.3 India's White Revolution and Increased Milk Availability

The White Revolution turned India, once a major importer of milk, into the world's biggest producer of milk (Figure 2.5). Since the early 1970s, milk production in India has increased six-fold, from about 20 million tonnes to over 120 million tonnes. What makes this huge growth of the dairy sector unique is that it is based on small-scale, household-level milk production, and a massive network of marketing and service cooperatives. India's Operation Flood, as the public programme for organizing the dairy sector was called, envisaged organizing small, household-level dairy farmers into a structure of village-, district- and State-level cooperatives. Milk produced by small-scale dairy farmers is procured by village-level dairy cooperatives and transported to a district-level milk union, where it is processed and then marketed through a State-level federation of dairy unions (Kurien, 2004). Starting from a single district in Gujarat State, over the last four decades, about 15 million dairy farmers have been organized through 150,000 village-level primary cooperatives and 183 district-level unions.

FIGURE 2.5 India: Growth of milk availability and cooperative dairy sector, 1950–51 to 2011–12

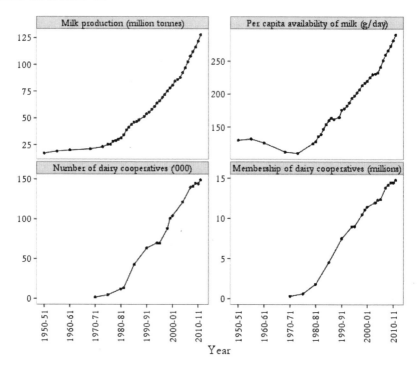

The organization of small-scale producers under the umbrella of State-level federations and district-level unions has facilitated dissemination of state-of-the-art technical services. Dairy farmers and other workers were provided with modern equipment and trained in hygienic work practices to ensure uncontaminated production, collection, and distribution. Modern veterinary services were made available through the network of cooperatives.

Cross-breeding was facilitated by training leading dairy farmers in thousands of villages to provide artificial insemination services. Currently, about 50 million cattle are cross-bred annually using artificial insemination (www.nddb.org/English/Statistics/Pages/Performed-States.aspx). Cross-breeding has resulted in significant increases in the milk yield of cattle (Gautam, Dalal, and Pathak, 2010). The increased supply of feed concentrates, from about 1.7 thousand tonnes per day in the 1970s to about 5.2 thousand tonnes per day in 2002, also helped raise the milk yield of the animals.

It was recognized early that providing remunerative prices to dairy farmers was critical for growth in the sector (Jha *et al.*, 1984). An important aspect of the policy was to provide remunerative prices to dairy farmers through fat-based pricing of milk. Inexpensive techniques for measurement of fat content facilitated scaling up procurement using fat content as the basis for pricing, while discouraging the dilution and adulteration of milk.

Milk processing plants set up at the level of district unions allowed for cold storage as well as drying of milk. Drying milk during the peak seasons and its reconstitution during the lean summer months not only helped reduce seasonal variations in milk supply, but also facilitated transportation from regions of surplus production to regions of low supply. Insulated train wagons and refrigerated trucks have also been used to build a National Milk Grid to transport milk from regions of surplus to regions of deficit (Cunningham, 2009).

The huge expansion of the dairy sector in India has facilitated a significant increase in the availability and consumption of milk and dairy products in India. Since Operation Flood was launched, the per capita availability of milk has almost tripled, from about 110 grams per capita per day to about 290 grams per capita per day (Figure 2.5). According to data from the consumer expenditure surveys conducted by the National Sample Survey Organization (NSSO) in India, average milk consumption increased from about 45 kilograms per capita per annum in 1983 to about 57 kilograms per capita per annum in 2009–10 (Table 2.2).

TABLE 2.2 India: Average consumption of milk, kg per capita per annum

Year	Rural	Urban	All
1983	38.7	55.6	44.7
1993–1994	50.3	66.4	54.3
2004–2005	50.2	69.3	55
2009–2010	51.7	71.6	57.1

Source: Kumar *et al.* (2014)

Given the very low consumption of other animal-source foods in India, milk is an important source of protein in Indian diets. By empowering small producers, Operation Flood led to a very impressive expansion of the dairy sector. This has had extremely important implications, not only for incomes of dairy farmers in India, but for overall levels of nutrition in the country.

Box 2.4 Home Gardens Significantly Improve Diet Diversity

Across the world, home gardens have been an important source of nutritious food. Home gardens are agro-forestry units in which a combination of trees, seasonal crops, and animals are raised (Fernandes and Nair, 1986). Households can produce a variety of foods by maintaining home gardens in marginal spaces on or adjacent to homesteads. Proximity to home facilitates the tending of kitchen gardens and helps minimize loss of nutrients due to storage and transportation, as freshly plucked fruits and vegetables can be used as household food.

Home gardens only require modest financial resources and can be maintained using the household's own idle labour (Jacob, 2014). Being on or adjacent to homesteads, in many regions, home gardens are primarily maintained by women, who combine work on the gardens with other household chores. In India, national statistics for 2011–12 show that about a quarter of rural women who were principally engaged in housework and about 8 percent of urban women principally engaged in housework regularly maintained home gardens (Rawal and Saha, 2015).

Studies across the world show that home gardens are *in situ* repositories of considerable biodiversity. Fernandes and Nair (1986) point out that plant diversity is a characteristic feature of home gardens across different ecological and social contexts. A study of about 300 home gardens in Java, Indonesia, recorded over 500 different plant species. A study of twenty home gardens in Nicaragua found a total of 324 species (Méndez, Lok, and Somarriba, 2001). A study of a Peruvian village recorded 168 species in twenty one home gardens (Padoch and De Jong, 1991). A study of 134 home gardens in Nepal found a total of 165 crop species (Sunwar *et al.*, 2006). In a study of 400 home gardens in Kerala, India, Jacob (1997) found that the number of plant species in a typical four-tier home garden ranged from five to forty. A study of 80 Mayan home gardens in Mexico recorded 150 different species (DeClerck and Negreros-Castillo, 2000). Okafor and Fernandes (1987) found that home gardens in Nigeria, comprising trees, shrubs, agricultural crops, and small livestock, were germplasm banks for a large number of plant species disappearing outside those spaces.

Fernandes and Nair (1986) point out that among trees, fruit trees dominate home gardens across ecological settings: "while the fruit trees such as guava, rambutan, mango, mangosteen, and so on, along with other food-producing trees such as *Moringa* sp. and *Sesbania grandiflora*, dominate the Asian home gardens, indigenous trees that produce leafy vegetables (*Pterocarpus* spp.), fruit for cooking (*Dacroydes edulis*), condiment (*Pentaclethra macrophylla*), and so on, dominate the West African compound farms". Given this rich biodiversity, produce from home gardens not only makes a significant contribution to the food consumption of households, but is also particularly important for dietary diversity.

In many countries, projects supporting home gardening, by providing seeds for a diverse variety of plants, other inputs and credit, and through awareness and training programmes among households, have brought considerable benefit in terms of nutritional outcomes. Distribution of homesteads as part of the land reform programme in West Bengal, India, resulted in greater use of homesteads for growing fruits and vegetables, fish-farming in small homestead ponds, and maintenance of small animals on homesteads.

TABLE 2.3 Biodiversity in home gardens in selected countries of the world

Location	Major food crops	Livestock type
Java, Indonesia	Upland rice, maize, vegetables, coconut, fruit trees	Poultry, fish, goats, sheep, cows, water buffalo
Philippines	Sweet potatoes, coconut, banana	Poultry, pigs
South Pacific Islands	Coconut, colocasia, yams, arrowroot	No data
Sri Lanka		Poultry
Kerala, India	Tuber crops, upland rice, banana, vegetables	Poultry, cattle
Southeast Nigeria	Yams, cocoyam, banana	Goats, sheep, poultry
Northern Tanzania	Banana, beans, colocasia, xanthosoma, yams	Cattle, goats, pigs, poultry
Burkina Faso	Maize, red sorghum	Goats, sheep, poultry
Tabasco, Mexico	Maize, beans	Poultry, pigs, sheep and goats
Grenada, West Indies	Colocasia, xanthosoma, yams, maize, pigeon peas	

Source: Based on Fernandes and Nair (1986).

Evidence from many countries has shown that maintenance of home gardens is associated with improved intake of nutrients and improved nutritional outcomes. Berti, Krasevec, and FitzGerald (2004) systematically reviewed evidence on the impact of agricultural interventions in Africa, Asia, and the Americas on nutrition. Of the thirty projects reviewed by them, eighteen were home gardening (vegetable and livestock) projects. In all the home gardening projects, improvements in diet were recorded. Of the six home gardening projects where anthropometric indicators were monitored, three recorded significant improvements. In seven studies where biochemical/clinical indicators were monitored, four recorded improvements in biochemical/clinical indicators for different types of micronutrient deficiencies on account of home gardens. Talukder *et al.* (2010) evaluated the impact of homestead gardening programmes in Bangladesh, Cambodia, Philippines, and Nepal, and found improved diets among households that participated in these programmes, resulting in faster reduction of anaemia among children from such households compared to children from control households.

covering studies from many developed countries. They used energy density (defined as calories available per unit weight of food) as a negative measure of diet quality (that is, the higher the energy density, the poorer the quality of diet). Their review showed that better socio-economic conditions, as reflected in occupational status, level of education and incomes, are associated with greater consumption of foods with low energy density and high vitamin and mineral content, such as whole grains, lean meat, fish, fruits, and vegetables. On the other hand, the diets of persons belonging to the lower socio-economic categories consist of food that is "energy-dense but nutrient-poor". Darmon and Drewnowski (2008) point out that other studies using multidimensional indices of diet quality have also found similar relationships between diet quality and economic conditions.

Recent evidence from the United States and the United Kingdom suggests that disparities in quality of diet across socio-economic groups may even have intensified over time. A recent widely cited study of diet quality in the United States shows that persons with relatively high socio-economic status have more diverse and nutritious diets than those with relatively low socio-economic status, and that the diet gap between the rich and the poor has increased between 1999 and 2010 (Wang *et al.*, 2014). The study used a multidimensional Alternate Healthy Eating Index to measure diet quality, and found a positive relationship of diet quality with family income and education levels. Using income and educational levels, it classified the sample into two categories by socio-economic status. The study found that while the diet quality of the group classified as having high socio-economic status improved significantly between 1999–2000 and 2009–10, no significant trend was seen in the diet quality of the low-socio-economic status group (Wang *et al.*, 2014).

Empirical evidence clearly shows that energy-dense foods such as refined grains, sugars and fats are the cheapest sources of dietary energy, while fruits and vegetables are the most expensive sources of dietary energy (Andrieu, Darmon, and Drewnowski, 2006; Darmon, Briend, and Drewnowski, 2004; Drewnowski, 2010; Drewnowski and Darmon, 2005). Table 2.4 gives data on the average energy density of different food groups. These data clearly show that energy-dense foods – grain products, fats, and sugars – have the lowest unit cost of calories. Compared to grains, fats and sugars, on average, animal-source foods have lower energy density and higher energy cost. Fruits and vegetables have the lowest energy density and highest energy cost. Data on energy costs from France presented in Table 2.5 also show similar ranking for different food items. While human diets also have social and cultural determinants, the high energy cost of foods with low energy density is the most important reason why the diets of low-income households consist of very low quantities of nutritious food commodities. Evidence on the costs of different types of diets in South Africa is similar (Temple and Steyn, 2009, 2011; Temple *et al.*, 2011). Table 2.6, taken from Jones *et al.* (2014), shows that, in the United Kingdom, the average price per unit of dietary energy from fruits and vegetables was £ 9.13/1000 kcal, while one could get 1000 kcal of dietary energy by spending only £ 1.26 on bread, potatoes, and pasta. Detailed statistical analysis presented by Jones *et al.* (2014) shows that the price gap between less healthy food items and their more healthy alternatives had increased in the United Kingdom between 2002 and 2012.

Evidence from developing countries also shows significant differences in the pattern of food consumption across different economic classes. Data from household consumer expenditure surveys of developing countries show that cereals dominate the food consumption of the poor, while more affluent households spend a greater share of their food expenditure on food of animal origin (meat, fish, eggs, and milk). Tables 2.7–2.10 show these patterns for Indonesia, Malaysia, South Africa, and India. Table 2.7 shows that, in both rural and urban Indonesia, the share of cereals and tubers declines as one goes from the poorest expenditure class to the higher expenditure classes, while the share of animal-source high-protein food rises. According to the 2009–10 Household Expenditure Survey in Malaysia, the share of animal-source foods in total household food expenditure increased from 39 percent for the lowest two expenditure classes to 46 percent in the top five expenditure classes (Table 2.8). Table 2.9 shows a similar pattern for South Africa, with the share of animal-source foods rising from 32 percent for the poorest expenditure decile to 38 percent for the top decile.

Data for all four countries presented here show that, while the absolute quantity of consumption of fruits and vegetables rises as one goes from poor to more affluent households, the rise is considerably less than that for animal-source food. As a result, the share of fruits and vegetables in total consumption does not show any significant change across expenditure classes or deciles. In Indonesia, across most rural and urban expenditure classes, fruits and vegetables accounted for about 13–14 percent of food expenditure in 2013. In Malaysia, between 15–17 percent of food expenditure was on fruits and vegetables by households in all expenditure classes. In South Africa, expenditure on fruits and vegetables accounted for about 12–14 percent of total food expenditure in each expenditure decile. In India, fruits and vegetables accounted for about 17 percent of total food expenditure in each fractile class in both rural and urban areas.

TABLE 2.4 United States: Average energy density and price per unit of dietary energy for different food groups, 2001–02

Food groups	Energy density (kcal/100 g)	Water content (gms/100 g)	Serving size (g)	Price (US$ per 100 g)	Price (US$ per serving)	Energy cost (US$/100 kcal)
Milk and milk products	182	66	112	0.4	0.26	0.23
Meat, poultry, and fish	224	60	89	0.8	0.63	0.41
Eggs	171	72	65	0.32	0.24	0.22
Dry beans, legumes, nuts and seeds	330	40	76	0.5	0.26	0.18
Grain products	337	24	63	0.47	0.23	0.14
Fruit	67	82	157	0.28	0.4	0.54
Vegetables	83	80	102	0.33	0.29	0.68
Fats, oils, and salad dressings	390	47	22	0.37	0.09	0.17
Sugars, sweets and beverages	242	45	119	0.4	0.23	0.22

Source: Drewnowski (2010).

TABLE 2.5 France: Price per unit of dietary energy from different food items, 2000

Food group	Food item (energy cost, €/MJ)
Meats	Red meat (1.23), lean meat (2.17), poultry (1.14), liver (0.73), organ meats (0.93), pork (2.29), lunch meats (0.39), eggs (0.42), fresh fish (3.92), canned fish (0.98), shellfish (3.61)
Fruit and vegetables	Potatoes (0.30), root vegetables (0.92), peas and beans (0.79), pulses (0.04), mixed vegetables (3.18), leafy vegetables (4.89), tomatoes (3.84), fresh fruit (1.17), nuts (0.09), dried fruit (0.41), canned fruit (0.38), 100% fruit juice (0.51), citrus fruit (1.49), bananas/raisins/figs (0.59)
Dairy	Whole milk (0.31), low-fat milk (0.30), skimmed milk (0.34), yoghurt (0.78), fruit yoghurt (0.35), pudding (0.33), uncured cheese 40% fat (0.41), uncured cheese 20% fat (0.52), uncured cheese 0% fat (0.84), hard cheese (0.50), soft cheese (0.48)
Grains	Bread (0.26), whole-grain bread (0.34), rolls (0.15), breakfast cereal (0.32), pasta/rice (0.13), bakery goods (0.26), crackers (0.19), pastries (0.38), cookies (0.14)
Fats and sweets	Butter (0.18), light butter (0.36), cream (0.22), oil (0.04), margarine (0.09), sugar (0.08), chocolate (0.30), hard candy (0.33), syrup (0.20), honey/jam (0.22), carbonated beverages (0.48), cocoa powder (0.15)

Source: Darmon, Briend, and Drewnowski (2004).

TABLE 2.6 United Kingdom: Average price per unit of dietary energy from different food groups, 2012

Food group	Average price (£/1000 kcal)
Bread, rice potatoes, pasta	1.26
Fruits and vegetables	9.13
Milk and dairy foods	4.75
Meat, fish, eggs, beans and other sources of protein	4.93
Food and drinks high in fat and/or sugar	3.11

Source: Jones et al. (2014).

TABLE 2.7 Indonesia: Share of selected commodity groups in total food expenditure, by monthly per capita expenditure class, rural and urban, 2013 (percent)

Monthly per capita expenditure class (Rupiah)	Rural			Urban		
	Cereals and tubers	Fish, meat, eggs and milk	Fruits and vegetables	Cereals and tubers	Fish, meat, eggs and milk	Fruits and vegetables
Less than 100000	54	9	14	59	8	10
100000–149999	48	10	13	47	9	13
150000–199999	41	11	14	40	11	13
200000–299999	32	13	14	31	13	14
300000–499999	25	15	14	23	15	14
500000–749999	20	17	14	18	17	14
750000–999999	17	19	14	15	20	14
1000000 and over	13	21	14	10	20	13
All	22	16	14	17	18	13

Source: Badan Pusat Statistik (www.bps.go.id/eng/tab_sub/view.php?kat=1tabel=1daftar=1id_subyek=05notab=40) and www.bps.go.id/eng/tab_sub/view.php?kat=1tabel=1daftar=1id_subyek=05notab=38

TABLE 2.8 Malaysia: Share of selected commodity groups in total household food expenditure, by monthly household expenditure class, 2009–10 (percent)

Household expenditure class (Ringgit Malaysia)	Cereals	Fish, meat, eggs, and milk	Fruits and vegetables
Less than RM 500	30	39	15
RM 500–599	29	39	16
RM 600–699	28	40	16
RM 700–799	27	42	16
RM 800–899	26	42	16
RM 900–999	25	43	16
RM 1000–1999	22	46	17
RM 2000–2999	21	46	17
RM 3000–3999	20	46	16
RM 4000–4999	19	46	17
RM 5000 and above	19	46	16

Source: Household Expenditure Survey, 2009–10, Department of Statistics, Government of Malaysia.

TABLE 2.9 South Africa: Share of selected commodity groups in total food expenditure, by deciles of monthly per capita expenditure, 2010–11 (percent)

Expenditure decile	Cereals	Meat, fish, eggs, and milk	Fruits and vegetables
1	34	32	14
2	34	32	13
3	33	32	13
4	31	33	12
5	31	33	12
6	29	35	12
7	26	38	12
8	23	41	12
9	18	43	13
10	14	38	13
All	24	37	13

Source: Statistics South Africa (2012).

TABLE 2.10 India: Share of selected commodity groups in total food expenditure, by fractile classes of monthly per capita expenditure, rural and urban, 2011–12 (percent)

Fractile class of monthly per capita expenditure	Rural			Urban		
	Cereals	Meat, fish, eggs and milk	Fruits and vegetables	Cereals	Meat, fish, eggs and milk	Fruits and vegetables
1	32.6	10.0	17.8	28.6	15.0	17.1
2	30.2	13.4	17.4	24.2	19.1	16.6
3	28.2	16.7	17.2	22.5	21.9	16.3
4	26.1	18.6	17.3	20.5	24.0	16.6
5	24.4	20.9	16.7	18.8	25.4	16.8
6	22.6	22.1	16.7	17.7	25.7	16.8
7	21.4	23.8	16.5	17.0	26.4	17.6
8	20.0	24.9	16.6	15.9	26.6	17.8
9	18.8	26.0	16.9	14.9	26.7	17.7
10	17.1	28.2	16.8	13.5	27.1	17.6
11	15.1	29.8	17.2	11.5	26.2	17.5
12	12.2	30.1	15.8	7.9	21.7	15.4
All	20.3	24.2	16.8	15.6	25.0	17.1

Source: NSSO (2014).

It is arguable that the lack of a positive relationship between the share of expenditure on fruits and vegetables with economic status in low- and middle-income countries is because the unit cost of calories from fruits and vegetables is considerably higher than the cost of calories from even animal-source foods. As a result, in low- and middle-income countries, although the absolute intake of fruits and vegetables rises with economic conditions, even households with relatively higher economic status cannot afford to adequately substitute the intake of calorie-rich food with greater intake of fruits and vegetables. As a result, the share of food expenditure for fruits and vegetables remains very low for all economic classes.

Other determinants of diet quality

Diets and consumption patterns are also affected by non-economic factors, including the social and cultural context, health and dietary awareness among consumers, as well as the influence of advertising. Although there is a positive relationship between economic status and quality of diet, inadequate consumption of nutritious foods like fruits and vegetables and dietary imbalances are found among high-income consumers as well. Energy-dense foods are rich in fats and sugars, which make the food more palatable, and results in lack of satiation and satiety as their consumption is reduced (Drewnowski, 1998). This in turn results in a considerable degree of resistance to the substitution of energy-dense food despite consumer awareness, and even when more nutritious foods are available and affordable. Systematic reviews of evidence find that food advertisements primarily focus on energy-dense food high in fat, salt, and sugar, and that such food advertising has a strong influence on diets, particularly of children (Cairns, Angus, and Hastings, 2009; Hastings *et al.*, 2006). It is now widely recognized that improving dietary choices requires combining nutrition education and public information campaigns with regulation of exposure of children to unhealthy food advertisements. In view of the harmful effects of food advertising on the diets of children, the Sixty-third World Health Assembly endorsed a set of recommendations for member-states to regulate marketing of foods and non-alcoholic beverages to children.[3]

Key messages

Improving economic and physical access to nutritious foods that have low energy density and are rich in nutrients is critical for alleviating malnutrition.

---

[3] Set of Recommendations on the marketing of foods and non-alcoholic beverages to children, WHA63.14 Resolution of the Sixty-third World Health Assembly adopted on 21 May 2010, World Health Organization, Geneva; available at whqlibdoc.who.int/publications/2010/9789241500210_eng.pdf?ua=1.

This requires that all rural and urban households have sufficient incomes not only to be able to access adequate quantities of foodgrains, but also nutritious diets. Rural households need access to land and other productive resources to support their livelihood, and to produce adequate and nutritious food, not just to feed themselves but other consumers as well.

It is also important that food price volatility is kept under control, and that food prices remain affordable and food production remunerative.

Sustainability of food systems

Much food output augmentation in the past has put increasing stress on natural resources – degrading the soil, polluting and exhausting fresh-water supplies, encroaching on forests, depleting wild fish stocks, and reducing biodiversity. More intensive farming systems and continued deforestation for agriculture and other land uses have also become major sources of greenhouse gas emission, particularly in industrialized countries. Harvest and post-harvest food losses, particularly in developing countries, as well as high food wastage at the end of the food chain, particularly in middle- and high-income countries, reduce food availability (FAO, 2011a).

While our approach to food production has become unsustainable, we have the means to transform our production systems and consumption patterns to create better food systems, to ensure healthier people. FAO (2014) provides a conceptual framework for the development of sustainable food systems, based on the following key principles.

1. Improving efficiency in the use of resources is crucial to sustainable agriculture.

2. Sustainability requires direct actions to conserve, protect, and enhance natural resources.

3. Agriculture that fails to protect and improve rural livelihoods, equity, and social well-being is unsustainable.

4. Enhanced resilience of people, communities, and ecosystems is key to sustainable agriculture.

5. Sustainable food and agriculture requires responsible and effective governance mechanisms.

Creating more resilient food systems that take into account the special needs of the more vulnerable is the most practical, cost-efficient, and sustainable way to address all forms of malnutrition. We need to produce nutritious food for all people today, while also protecting the capacity of future generations to feed themselves. Nutrition must become one of the primary objectives of food-system policies and interventions, ensuring access to an adequate, diverse, and balanced combination of dietary energy and nutrients.

At every stage along the way, resources must be used more efficiently and with less adverse impacts. Getting more and better food from water, land, fertilizer, and labour can save resources and make food systems more sustainable. An additional challenge is to manage livestock production (in particular, large, industrial-scale) sustainably, since it contributes more to greenhouse gases, resource consumption, disease transmission, and health problems due to excessive meat consumption.

Consumption of meat, milk, and eggs is growing rapidly in developing countries, providing nutritious diets to previously food-insecure populations. The livestock sector also improves livelihoods and contributes to economic growth and rural incomes. We must manage this sector sustainably, fostering a balanced, participatory, and consultative process among key stakeholders.

Supporting smallholder agriculture to make it more nutrition-sensitive

There is increasing recognition that agriculture must be more "nutrition-sensitive", with agricultural policies and practices supporting and facilitating more healthy – nutritionally adequate and diverse – diets.

Improving the productivity of small-scale farms while promoting diversification and more sustainable practices can reduce rural malnutrition by improving the local availability and nutritional quality of food, as well as by raising incomes and access to better food. This typically requires investments in public goods, including physical and social infrastructure, public support for agricultural research and extension, and ensuring that agricultural production, particularly by smallholder producers, remains profitable. Improving access to land, finance, productive assets, technology, input and output markets, as well as other supportive measures generally enhances small producers' productivity, income, spending, and nutrition.

To make agriculture more nutrition-sensitive, attention must be paid to supporting mixed farming systems, protecting on-farm biodiversity, and promoting production of nutritious but underutilized crops (Mayes *et al.*, 2011). Agricultural research and development must focus more intensely on nutrient-dense foods, such as millets, legumes, fruits, vegetables, and animal-source foods, as well as on local biodiversity and diversified farming systems. Research to develop new varieties and to increase the yields of many of these nutrient-dense crops has not been prioritized historically. It is essential to correct this imbalance in agricultural research.

Making agriculture nutrition-sensitive is essential for a sustainable approach to addressing micronutrient deficiencies, and represents both a challenge and an important economic opportunity for agriculture.

Box 2.5 ICN2 Framework for Action: Recommended actions for sustainable food systems promoting healthy diets

- Recommendation 8: Review national policies and investments and integrate nutrition objectives into food and agriculture policy, programme design and implementation, to enhance nutrition sensitive agriculture, ensure food security and enable healthy diets.

- Recommendation 9: Strengthen local food production and processing, especially by smallholder[a] and family farmers, giving special attention to women's empowerment, while recognizing that efficient and effective trade is key to achieving nutrition objectives.

- Recommendation 10: Promote the diversification of crops including underutilized traditional crops, more production of fruits and vegetables, and appropriate production of animal-source products as needed, applying sustainable food production and natural resource management practices.

- Recommendation 11: Improve storage, preservation, transport and distribution technologies and infrastructure to reduce seasonal food insecurity, food and nutrient loss and waste.

- Recommendation 12: Establish and strengthen institutions, policies, programmes and services to enhance the resilience of the food supply in crisis-prone areas, including areas affected by climate change.

- Recommendation 13: Develop, adopt and adapt, where appropriate, international guidelines on healthy diets.

- Recommendation 14: Encourage gradual reduction of saturated fat, sugars and salt/sodium and trans-fat from foods and beverages to prevent excessive intake by consumers and improve nutrient content of foods, as needed.

- Recommendation 15: Explore regulatory and voluntary instruments – such as marketing, publicity and labelling policies, economic incentives or disincentives in accordance with Codex Alimentarius and World Trade Organization rules – to promote healthy diets.

- Recommendation 16: Establish food or nutrient-based standards to make healthy diets and safe drinking water accessible in public facilities such as hospitals, childcare facilities, workplaces, universities, schools, food and catering services, government offices and prisons, and encourage the establishment of facilities for breastfeeding.

---

[a] Smallholder farmers include agriculture and food workers, artisanal fisherfolk, pastoralists, indigenous peoples and the landless (Committee on World Food Security, Global Strategic Framework for Food Security and Nutrition, 2013).

3

Social Protection against Food Insecurity and Malnutrition

Experience shows that some initiatives for eradicating hunger and malnutrition require special efforts by national governments in order to accelerate progress. Social protection is clearly one such area.

Social protection can ensure access to a minimum level of resources so that people can have decent conditions of work and life. In recent years, discussions on social protection have moved towards the idea of providing a social protection floor, which refers to a set of nationally determined basic social security guarantees for everyone. The General Conference of the International Labour Organization (ILO) adopted the Social Protection Floors Recommendation in 2012, which identified four sets of basic guarantees that any national social protection floor should include: (a) access to essential health care; (b) income security for children, ensuring access to adequate nutrition, education, and care; (c) basic income security for persons of active working age unable to earn a sufficient income; and (d) basic income security for older persons.

Guarantee against food insecurity and malnutrition is thus a crucial component of a social protection floor. In this context, discussions on the Right to Food and implementation of FAO's Voluntary Guidelines to Support the Progressive Realization of the Right to Adequate Food in the Context of National Food Security are central (Ajemian, 2014; De Schutter, 2014; FAO, 2005).

Social protection is provided in various forms. These include cash or in-kind transfer payments, subsidized provision of goods and services, insurance, and guarantee of wages and employment. Although there are variations in the efficacy of different types of programmes depending on the socio-economic context, in-kind transfer programmes, particularly when designed to meet minimum nutritional requirements of the target population, are an effective instrument for ending food insecurity and raising nutritional status. Cash transfer programmes, with substantial benefits and broad coverage, can also provide complementary resources in the hands of households to buy food and to invest in food production.

Why is social protection important for food security and nutrition?

A system of social protection not only protects the vulnerable against economic and environmental shocks, but also ensures that everyone has enough resources to be able to acquire adequate nutritious food. Social protection can significantly reduce income poverty in rural areas. Complementary social protection programmes can target specific nutritional deficiencies and vulnerable population groups. These include children, pregnant and lactating mothers, older persons, and persons belonging to disadvantaged social or occupational groups.

Social protection programmes also have positive spill-over effects such as by creating upward pressure on wages, enhancing small producers' accumulation of productive resources, and increasing productivity, infrastructural development, and augmenting demand. A significant impact of social protection is improving access of poor producers to investible resources. FAO's *From Protection to Production* studies have shown that social protection programmes can significantly boost agricultural as well as non-agricultural production (Box 3.1). Over time, a well-functioning social protection system can significantly support rural livelihoods and help improve the nutritional status of the population at large.

Social protection for the poor also helps augment demand, which in turn can have very substantial multiplier effects on domestic production and national income. The impact of social protection on demand can be crucial in times of economic crises. This was witnessed in many countries during the post-2008 financial crisis. Discussing the role of social protection during the financial crisis, a report of the Social Protection Floor Advisory Group (ILO, 2012) concluded: "Recent years have provided potent proof of the value of social protection interventions in a time of crisis. Throughout the economic and financial crisis many floor-type social protection measures acted as effective counter-cyclical stabilizers. They helped attenuate the adverse impact on labour markets, contributed to maintaining social cohesion and stimulated aggregate demand. The combined effect of this effort ultimately aided and spurred economic recovery in a range of countries."

Public expenditure for social protection varies considerably across countries according to the extent of coverage and the level of social protection provided. While it is desirable that countries progressively expand the coverage and extent of social protection, and increase public expenditure on social protection to facilitate that, it has been pointed out that the extent of social protection benefits can be substantial even with relatively modest fiscal outlays. The ILO has estimated that 6 percent of global GDP is required to provide basic social security cover to all those without access to social security. It has been argued that this should be possible by primarily using national resources (ILO, 2008). Three-quarters of the world's poorest people live in rural areas, and many are themselves producers of food. Historically, social protection has emerged in urban areas, primarily for wage employees, military veterans, and the unemployed. Extending social protection to the countryside requires a major reorientation and reorganization of social protection. It is also important to orient social protection to enhance the productive and income-generating capacities and capabilities of the beneficiaries.

Provision of food through social protection programmes

Direct provisioning of food is done through various kinds of social protection programmes. These include food assistance programmes, programmes that provide subsidized food, school-meal programmes and other programmes where cooked food is provided to particularly vulnerable sections of the population, and food-for-work programmes. Food provisioning programmes have historically been an important part of the food security policies of many countries. Programmes for provision of free or subsidized food were used in many developing countries during much of the twentieth century. The use of food-for-work programmes to create demand as well as build public infrastructure also has a very long history.

Trends in food provisioning programmes

Over the last few decades, many countries have discontinued large food provisioning programmes and shifted to other forms of social protection. There were three primary drivers of this change. First, international finance institutions, donors, and other advocates of fiscal conservatism criticized food subsidy programmes for being expensive. Food provisioning programmes in various countries were targets of reform under structural adjustment programmes implemented across the developing world. Secondly, since the early 1990s, global food aid has declined considerably (Barrett and Maxwell, 2005) and many international donors have shifted to supporting cash transfer programmes. While food aid declined and domestic production in developing countries grew slowly, food-deficit countries have had to rely on food imports. Globally, between 1980 and 2010, imports increased by 67 percent for wheat, 166 percent for rice, and 36 percent for maize. Thirdly, under the World Trade Organization's Uruguay Round agreement, procurement and stockholding of agricultural

Box 3.1 From Protection to Production: Linkages between Social Protection and Agricultural Production

The FAO's *From Protection to Production* project has systematically evaluated the impact of social protection programmes on income-generating activities and consumption in seven countries in Sub-Saharan Africa. All the programmes studied by the project are cash transfer programmes, targeting poor households. While transfers in some programmes under evaluation were unconditional, in other programmes, beneficiaries had to satisfy pre-specified conditions to be entitled to the transfers.

The project has developed a methodology called Local Economy-Wide Impact Evaluation (LEWIE) to assess the impact of these programmes on local economies. LEWIE uses local-level social accounting matrices for treatment and control households, created using household-, enterprise- and community-level survey data (Asfaw *et al.*, 2012).

The studies estimated that incomes generated on account of the cash transfer programmes were 1.27 to 2.52 times the amount of cash transferred (Table 3.1). The programmes accounted for 7 percent (Ghana) to 30 percent (Zambia) of per capita consumption of beneficiary households. The studies reported considerable improvement in the food security status of beneficiary households. In Zambia, Kenya, and Malawi, the studies reported increases in food expenditure and increased diversity of diets, particularly on account of increased consumption of animal-source foods. On the other hand, in Ghana and Lesotho, the unpredictability of transfers has meant that the programmes have had little impact on food expenditure and dietary diversity.

TABLE 3.1 Income multipliers of social protection programmes, by country

Country	Income multiplier
Ethiopia	
Hintalo-Wajirat	2.52
Abi-adi	1.35
Ghana	2.5
Lesotho	2.23
Malawi	1.27
Zambia	1.79
Zimbabwe	1.73

Source: Compiled from various reports of the PtoP Project.

Programmes were found to have had significant impact on various productive and income-generating activities (Table 3.2). Zambia's Child Grant Programme increased the extent of land cultivated, expenditure on agricultural inputs, and sale of crop and livestock products. In Lesotho and Ghana, the cash transfer programmes increased input use. In all the countries except Ghana, cash transfers were associated with increased ownership of different types of livestock. In Ghana, Malawi, and Zambia, cash transfers induced some beneficiary households to start non-agricultural business enterprises. In both Zambia and Malawi, cash transfers were associated with increased investment in agricultural implements.

TABLE 3.2 Production multipliers of social protection programmes, by country

Country	Crop production	Live-stock	Ser-vices	Non-agriculture	Retail
Ethiopia					
Hintalo-Wajirat	0.2	0.03	0.12	-0.14	1.35
Abi-adi	0	0.05	0.02	0	1.25
Ghana	0.27	0.16	0.1	0.05	0.78
Lesotho	0.27	0.28	0.08	-0.01	0.59
Malawi	0.03	0.06	0.09	0.03	0.72
Zambia	0.47	0.09	0.28	0.02	1.91
Zimbabwe	0.31	0.14	-0.54	0	0.6

Source: Compiled from various reports of the PtoP Project.

products through domestic price support programmes were classified as trade-distorting and severely restricted. Consequently, many developing countries switched from programmes providing subsidized food to other forms of assistance.

Given pressures to reduce the fiscal burden of social protection programmes, the shifts away from food provisioning programmes to other forms of social protection have also been associated with the narrowing of social protection.

Among developing countries, programmes for provision of subsidized food are now limited to a few large countries that are able to fiscally sustain their domestic procurement and distribution programmes. Of all the major ongoing food subsidy programmes, India's Public Distribution System (PDS) is arguably the largest. It provides subsidized grain to over 40 percent of Indian households. This was expected to be raised to two-thirds of the population under the National Food Security Act, 2013 (Box 3.2).

Another major food subsidy programme, Indonesia's Operasi Pasar Khusus Rice Subsidy Programme, was introduced in 1998. Under this programme, beneficiary households are entitled to get 10 kilograms of rice every month at a subsidized price (Tabor and Sawit, 2001). The programme, now called Rice for the Poor (Raskin), covers about 17 million households. It has been estimated that Raskin has reduced the probability of being poor among beneficiary households by about 4 percent (Sumarto, Suryahadi, and Widyanti, 2005). Raskin has not only increased rice consumption among beneficiaries, but also allowed them to consume greater quantities of other nutritious food items including meat, fish, and dairy products (Pangaribowo, 2012).

Box 3.2 Public Distribution System in India

Public distribution of foodgrains in India dates back to the inter-war period. The statutory wheat price was fixed for the first time in 1941. Much emphasis was put on producing more rice because of the decline in the supply of rice from Burma, which had been occupied by Japan. Before the 1960s, food distribution was based on imported food or food received in aid. By the 1970s, India became self-sufficient in the production of foodgrains and the Public Distribution System (PDS) evolved into a universal scheme for the distribution of subsidized food through a network of ration shops. Since the 1970s, the system of public procurement and the Public Distribution System (PDS) have functioned in tandem. A system of minimum support prices is used to provide incentives to farmers and to procure grain, which is then provided to consumers at subsidized prices under the PDS.

After India introduced structural adjustment programmes in the early 1990s, the principle of universal minimum entitlement was abandoned and coverage of the PDS progressively reduced (Swaminathan, 2000). In June 1992, geographical targeting was introduced under the Revamped PDS, with beneficiaries in specified backward and inaccessible blocks across the country being given higher grain entitlements than beneficiaries in the rest of the country. In 1997, different entitlements were introduced for households identified as below the poverty line (BPL) and for others, under the Targeted Public Distribution System (TPDS). Two changes were introduced in the PDS in 2000: first, the central government stopped subsidizing grain provided to households not classified as poor; and secondly, the central government introduced another category, of the poorest and most vulnerable, who were given greater grain entitlements at highly subsidized prices. On the other hand, with the introduction of differentiated entitlements, targeting was progressively narrowed and persons not identified as poor were excluded. It has been noted that the TPDS targets subsidies very narrowly, and a large proportion of food-insecure and vulnerable households are excluded from it.

The PDS is operated jointly by the central and State governments. The central government has the responsibility for procurement, storage, and provision of grains to the States. Using estimates of poverty, the central government specifies the quotas of each State for obtaining grain for different categories of beneficiaries. The States are provided grain at the central issue prices specified for each category of beneficiary. The State governments are responsible for the identification of the different target groups and the distribution of grain to them through a network of fair price shops. Given high food inflation around the end of the 2000s and large-scale exclusion of the poor from the TPDS, many State governments introduced additional subsidies and entitlements for different categories of beneficiaries in recent years. For example, Tamil Nadu re-introduced universal coverage of the PDS in 2006. In 2011, Chhattisgarh expanded the PDS under a State-level Food Security Act to provide subsidized grain to 90 percent of the population. While the introduction of narrow targeting has resulted in substantial exclusion of the poor and increased leakages from the programme, the expansion of its coverage in many States and the modernization of supply-chain management since the late 2000s have contributed to a very significant decline in leakages from the PDS, contributing to its remarkable revival (Drèze and Khera, 2015; Khera, 2011a, 2011b; Krishnamurthy, Pathania, and Tandon, 2014). Revival of the PDS has been associated with an increased proportion of households buying grain through PDS, rising from only 22 percent in 2004–05 to about 45 percent in 2011–12 (Himanshu and Sen, 2013).

As part of a larger move towards rights-based entitlements, the central government introduced the National Food Security Act (NFSA) in 2013 to revamp the TPDS (Ghosh, 2014; Sinha, 2013). Under the NFSA, 75 percent of the rural population and half of the urban population are entitled to subsidized grain. The NFSA promises to provide 5 kilograms of grain per person per month at subsidized prices to beneficiary households. An important feature of the NFSA is that it expanded the basket of grains to include millets and pulses, in addition to rice and wheat traditionally provided under the PDS. This is expected to have significant positive implications for nutritional outcomes. The NFSA also has specific provisions for nutritional support to pregnant and lactating women, as well as children.

India spends only about 1.2 percent of its GDP on the Public Distribution System (Ghosh, 2014). With a network of more than 462,000 fair price shops distributing grain annually to about 180 million households, India's PDS is the largest food distribution programme of its kind in the world. It also has been the most important instrument of India's public policy against poverty and undernourishment. According to large-scale survey data for 2009–10, the PDS was responsible for lifting 38 million people out of poverty in 2009–10 (Drèze and Khera, 2013; Himanshu and Sen, 2013). When fully implemented, the National Food Security Act is expected to further strengthen the PDS in dealing with food insecurity and malnutrition.

Brazil's food acquisition programme, Programa de Aquisição de Alimentos (PAA), is remarkable in many respects. The PAA, started in 2003 as part of the Fome Zero Programme, reorganized and expanded the earlier system of price support to farmers. Through the PAA, price support was extended to resource-poor family farmers. Figure 3.1 shows the large increase in number of beneficiaries and public expenditure on PAA between 2003 and 2012. The unique feature of the programme was that, besides procurement of central food stocks for price stabilization and food security, it also created marketing channels for local procurement of food through farmers' organizations and local networks for sale to locally food-insecure populations. Specific initiatives were taken to create opportunities for farmers to produce and sell vegetables, native fruits, grains, nuts, milk, and other nutritious food items. Food items procured from family farmers through the PAA were supplied to food-insecure households as well as to schools for their meal programmes (Peraci and Bittencourt, 2011; Silva et al., 2011; Soares et al., 2013; Swensson, 2015). Many assessments have shown that these initiatives have significantly improved the dietary diversity of both family farmers and food-insecure consumers (for reviews, see Grisa and Schmitt, 2013; Soares et al., 2013).

FIGURE 3.1 Brazil: Public expenditure on and number of beneficiary family farmers, Programa de Aquisição de Alimentos (PAA), Brazil, 2003–12

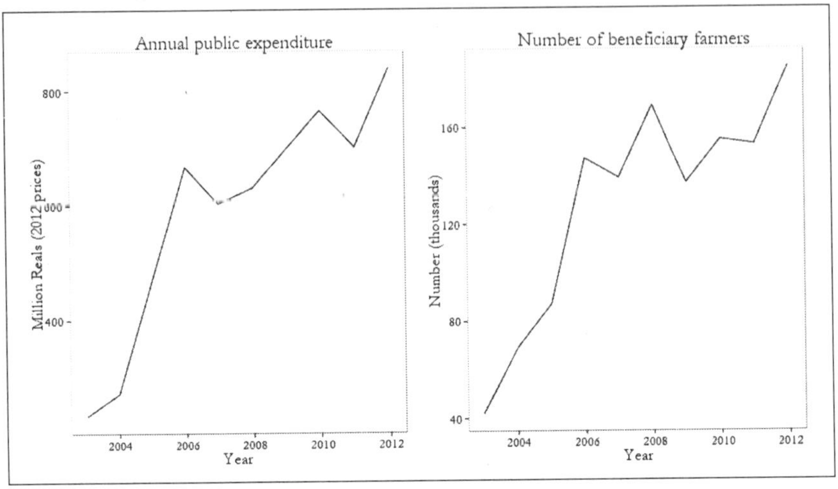

Source: Based on data from Soares et al. (2013).

Food assistance in emergencies

While many countries have discontinued general food provisioning programmes, it is common to use food provisioning to deal with disruption in food supplies because of disasters, emergencies and economic and humanitarian crises. For example, food assistance and food subsidies were relied upon by many countries to deal with the 2008 food price crisis. According to FAO's Global Information and Early Warning System for Food and Agriculture (GIEWS) database, five countries in Africa, five in Asia, and six in Latin America and the Caribbean instituted policy changes in favour of food subsidies/food assistance programmes in response to rising prices.[1] Of the ten African countries covered by the Monitoring and Analysing Food and Agricultural Policies (MAFAP) programme of FAO, six used distribution of subsidized food as a measure to deal with food price rises in 2008 (FAO, 2013a).

School feeding programmes

In contrast with the decline of programmes to subsidize food, food assistance in the form of school-meal programmes is being used more widely across countries (Figure 3.3). A World Food Programme report estimated that 368 million children the world over are fed in schools daily (World Food Programme, 2013). India's Mid-day Meal Scheme is the largest school

---

[1] www.fao.org/GIEWS/ENGLISH/policy/index.htm

FIGURE 3.2 Brazil: Public expenditure on and number of children provided meals through Programa Nacional de Alimentação Escolar (PNAE), 1995–2012

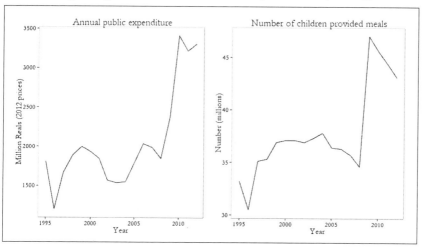

Source: Based on data from Soares et al. (2013) and Swensson (2015).

feeding programme in the world, feeding over 100 million children daily.

Brazil's school feeding programme, Programa Nacional de Alimentação Escolar (PNAE), feeds over 45 million children daily. The PNAE, which was started in 1954, saw a major expansion after its integration into the Fome Zero programme in 2003 (Figure 3.2). The PNAE is particularly noteworthy for the efforts taken to improve the nutritional quality of meals served. With its linkages to the Food Acquisition Programme (PAA), the PNAE has substantially increased inclusion of locally sourced fruits and vegetables in school meals. As a result, the proportion of schools in Brazil serving fruits in school meals increased from 28 percent in 2004 to 62 percent in 2006. Similarly, the proportion of schools serving fresh vegetables in school meals increased from 57 percent in 2004 to 80 percent in 2006, and to 90 percent in 2010 (Sidaner, Balaban, and Burlandy, 2013).

The European School Milk Scheme was started in the late 1970s to provide subsidized/free milk and dairy products to schoolchildren. In 2009–10, the European Union (EU) initiated a major programme to provide free fruit to children in schools. The scheme provides free fruit to over 8 million children in the EU. The EU covers 50–75 percent of the cost of fruit, with the rest borne by participating countries. In 2014, the EU merged its School Milk Scheme and its School Fruit Scheme into a single scheme (WHO, 2015).

Expanding the provision of food

Food subsidy and food assistance programmes are important instruments of social protection for improving access to food for the food-insecure and vulnerable. Such programmes directly result in increased food consumption, and thus have a direct impact on undernourishment and malnutrition.

Food-for-work programmes not only provide direct income support to manual wage earners, who are typically among the poorest sections in a country's population, but can also have an indirect effect on incomes by raising wage levels in labour markets. Food-for-work programmes can also make a significant contribution towards building public infrastructure. School-meal programmes have been shown to have a very positive impact on school enrolment as well as on the nutritional status of schoolchildren. School feeding programmes have also been used to mitigate the impact of various kinds of crises (Bundy *et al.*, 2009).

Food provisioning programmes, if based on procurement of food commodities from local farmers, can also support smallholder agriculture, promote production of more nutritious and less resource-intensive crops, and induce more sustainable land use. The 2013 *State of School Feeding Report* showed that, like all other food provisioning programmes, school feeding can help create demand for domestic agriculture. Local procurement of food not only helps increase demand for agriculture, but also facilitates the provision of diverse, nutritious, and unprocessed food to children (World Food Programme, 2013).

Food provisioning programmes based on domestic procurement of food can be designed to reduce the exposure of producers to price fluctuations and to ensure that they get decent remuneration through prices. Food provisioning programmes can also be used to induce dietary changes in favour of more nutritious food items.

A major advantage of entitlements specified in terms of food is that, unlike cash entitlements, food entitlements are automatically protected against food price inflation. This can be extremely important in times of high food-price inflation, which typically increases food insecurity.

It may also be pointed that food provisioning programmes, in general, have been popular among beneficiaries wherever they have been introduced in developing countries. Many studies from across different countries in Asia and Africa have reported preference of beneficiaries for in-kind provision (or a combination of cash and in-kind entitlements) over cash entitlements (Ahmed *et al.*, 2009; FAO, 2012; Ghosh, 2011; Hoddinott, Sandström, and Upton, 2013; Khera, 2011a; Sabates-Wheeler and Devereux, 2010).

Although food provisioning programmes have many advantages over other forms of social protection by ensuring access to adequate and nutritious food, the capacity of governments to run large-scale food distribution programme is limited by the World Trade Organization's Uruguay Round agreement. Public procurement of food from farmers through price support programmes is considered trade-distorting and classified in the Amber Box in WTO's current rules. Under these rules, the difference between prices offered to farmers under a public procurement programme and prices prevailing in 1986–88 is multiplied by the total output potentially eligible for support (not the actual quantity procured), to calculate the level of price support provided by a country. The price support thus computed is considered part of Amber Box subsidies, subject to restrictions on the Aggregate Measure of Support.

Over time, as world food prices have increased to levels far higher than the prices prevailing in 1986–88, the WTO restrictions on price support and public stockholdings have stifled food distribution programmes. On the other hand, these restrictions have done little to reduce the vast disparities between levels of support to agriculture provided by developed and developing countries. Despite restrictions imposed under the agreement, most developed countries have retained high levels of support for agriculture by shifting most of their subsidies to the unlimited "Green Box" of forms of support, not restricted by the Agreement on Agriculture. Green Box subsidies in developed countries, although not directly linked to levels of production, have helped farmers to innovate, invest, and increase productivity by providing additional resources for investment and by effectively reducing risks associated with investment. Such support has also extended social protection to the countryside. On the other hand, lacking comparable levels of support, cultivation by small producers in developing countries has become even less viable and uncompetitive. The WTO does not restrict Green Box-types of support to agriculture. However, administrative and other constraints limit the possibility and feasibility of developing countries using Green Box subsidies. The WTO provisions for policy instruments such as crop insurance to be counted in the Green Box are extremely restrictive. Green Box measures, such as decoupled payments – lump cash transfers to farmers – are not feasible in most developing countries because of domestic governance bottlenecks such as the absence of data, a lack of well-defined land titles, informal markets, frequent market failures, and insufficient rural financial facilities.

Restrictions on developing countries that provide support to smallholder producers and subsidized food to food-insecure consumers became the centre of a WTO dispute at the Bali Ministerial in 2013. India, which had just passed a National Food Security Act entitling two-thirds of its population to 5 kilograms of subsidized grains per capita per month through its food distribution programme, demanded relaxation of restrictions on such domestic price support programmes. The Bali agreement exempted existing programmes for stockholdings of traditional staple crops until a permanent solution to the dispute could be found. However, introduction of new food distribution programmes, expansion of existing programmes, and inclusion of nutritious non-staple foods in food distribution programmes continue to be subject to the Aggregate Measure of Support restrictions.

FIGURE 3.3 Proportion of children of primary and secondary school going age provided meals at school, by country, 2012 (percent)

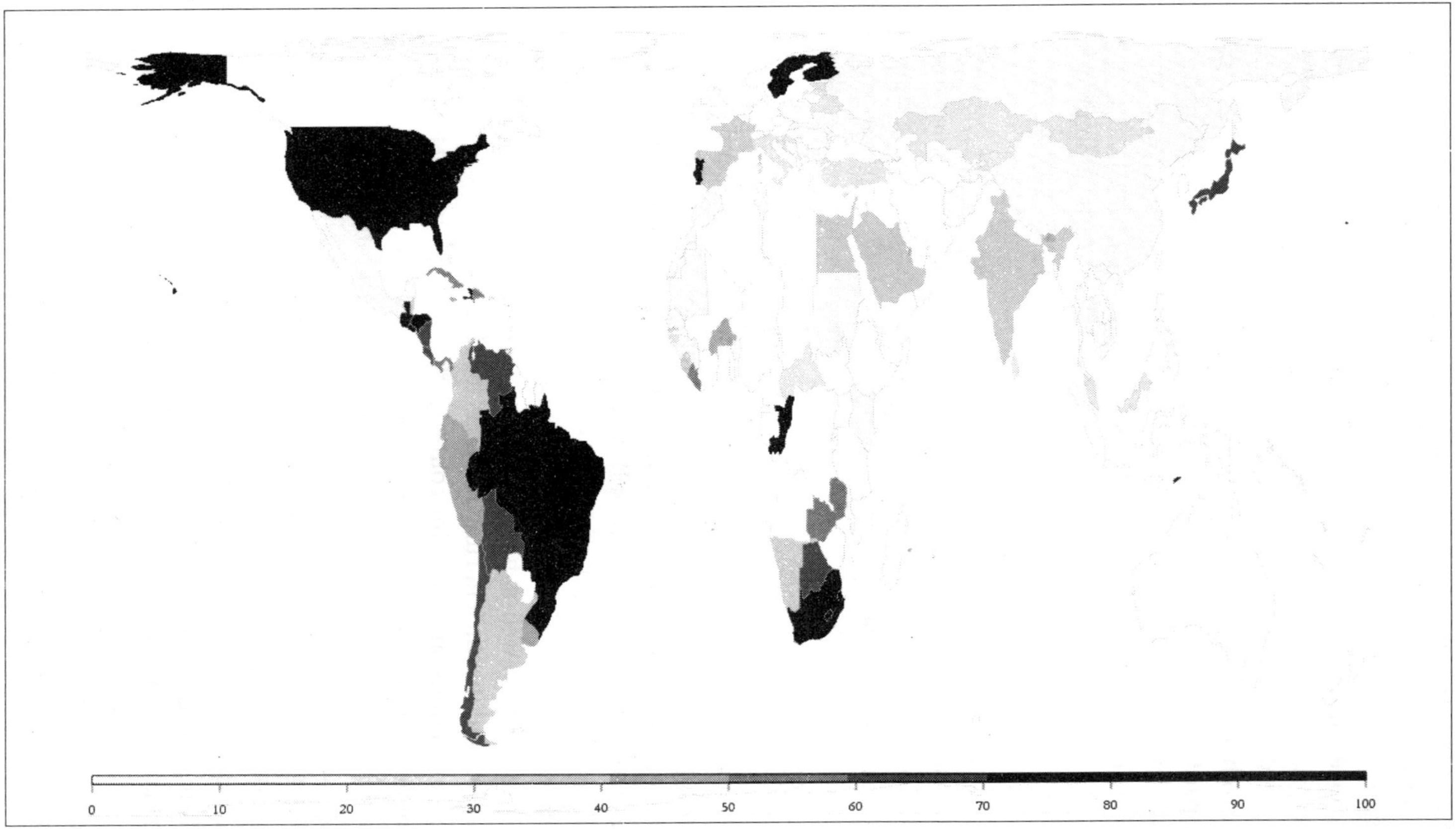

Note: Map plotted using Gall-Peters projection.
Source: Based on data on number of children covered in school feeding programmes from citet:schoolfood2013, and data on population of children of school going age from www.uis.unesco.org/DataCentre/Pages/BrowseEducation.aspx.

It is important that the global trade agreements are revised to remove disparities in permissible agricultural support levels between developed and developing countries, modify archaic clauses in the rules that govern global trade, and provide exemptions from restrictions on procurement programmes meant for domestic food security and support to poor producers. These rules have severely limited the potential of national governments to run food distribution programmes for the purpose of domestic food security.

Cash transfer programmes

Following the decline in food provisioning programmes over the last few decades and the recent promotion of cash transfer programmes, the latter have become the most widely used instrument for social protection in developing countries. Many countries, particularly in Latin America and the Caribbean, have established large-scale cash transfer programmes. Some of these have had remarkable outcomes in reducing the prevalence of poverty and food insecurity, though not necessarily malnutrition. Cash transfer programmes can be either conditional, when they require beneficiaries to satisfy certain conditions like sending children to school, or unconditional, where a basic transfer is ensured for all.

Cash transfer programmes in Latin America and the Caribbean

Large-scale use of conditional cash transfer (CCT) programmes started in Latin America in the late 1990s (Cecchini and Madariaga, 2011). By the end of the first decade of the twenty-first century, CCTs were used in almost all countries of Latin America and the Caribbean, covering about 19 percent of the region's population (Table 3.3). Spending on CCTs was about 0.4 percent of total GDP of all countries in the region. The most well-known and biggest CCT programme, Bolsa Familia in Brazil, started with a coverage of about 3.6 million families in 2003, when various social protection programmes in the country were merged to form the programme. By 2013, Bolsa Familia covered 13.9 million families. Mexico ended decades-old corn-tortilla subsidies and shifted to the Progresa-Oportunidades conditional cash transfer programme in the late 1990s. Starting with about 1.6 million families, the coverage of Progresa-Oportunidades expanded to about 5.8 million families by 2012.[2] In terms of coverage of national populations,

---

[2] In addition, about 700,000 households in Mexico were covered by the Programa de Apoyo Alimentario (PAL) in 2012. The PAL covers marginalized communities which cannot fulfil conditionalities of Oportunidades because of non-availability of schools and health facilities. Households covered by PAL can either opt to get a fixed food basket from the Distribuidora Compañía Nacional de Subsistencias Populares (DICONSA) store, or an equivalent amount of money.

TABLE 3.3 Latin America and the Caribbean: Coverage of and public expenditure on conditional cash transfer programmes, by country, 2009–10 (percent)

Country	Proportion of population covered	Expenditure on CCTs as % of GDP
Argentina	8.3	0.20
Bolivia	17.5	0.33
Brazil	26.4	0.47
Chile	6.8	0.11
Colombia	25.2	0.39
Costa Rica	3.3	0.39
Ecuador	44.3	1.17
El Salvador	8.2	0.02
Guatemala	22.6	0.32
Honduras	8.7	0.24
Jamaica	11.3	0.40
Mexico	24.6	0.51
Nicaragua	–	–
Panama	10.9	–
Paraguay	8.6	0.36
Peru	7.6	0.14
Dominican Republic	21.2	0.51
Trinidad and Tobago	2.4	0.19
Uruguay	11.6	0.45
Latin America and the Caribbean	19.3	0.40

Source: Based on data from Cecchini and Madariaga (2011).

Ecuador's Bono de Desarollo Humano programme has the highest coverage, of 44 percent.

Cash transfer programmes in Africa

While Latin American countries have been able to implement large-scale cash transfer programmes primarily with domestic resources, growth has been sporadic and slow in Africa. Social protection in Africa has been heavily dependent on aid and used primarily to deal with emergencies akin to 'social safety net' programmes. The decline in the availability of food aid has weakened social protection systems in Africa and encouraged countries to shift to donor-funded cash transfer programmes. Although a few middle-income countries have been able to sustain cash transfer programmes albeit with heavy donor support, in most African countries, cash transfer programmes have been implemented as pilot projects or as small, short-term projects to deal with emergencies. Kakwani, Soares, and

Son (2005) argue that owing to budgetary constraints, most cash transfer schemes in Africa set benefits at such low levels that they have very little impact on poverty.

Food stamps/coupons

Food stamps/coupons are essentially cash transfers only meant for food purchase. In a typical food coupon programme, beneficiaries are entitled to food coupons worth a specified amount of money every month, which they can use to buy food from approved retailers. Food retailers can then exchange these food coupons for money.

The longest running food stamps programme is the Food Stamps Programme in the United States, started by the Food Stamps Act of 1977 and renamed as the Supplementary Nutritional Assistance Programme in 2008, which covers, according to statistics for 2014–15, over 46 million Americans. By contrast, food coupons have not been very popular among developing countries (Josling, 2011). Most countries that have introduced food coupons have done so mainly to reduce the fiscal burden of food subsidies through narrow targeting. Several countries in Latin America and the Caribbean experimented with food coupons in the late 1970s and early 1980s, before abandoning them in favour of CCT programmes.

Since no producer subsidies are involved, food coupon programmes are not considered trade-distorting under the WTO's Uruguay Round Agreement on Agriculture.

Nutritional impact and limitations of cash transfer programmes

In countries that have implemented large cash transfer programmes – providing substantial transfers and covering most of their vulnerable population – these programmes have increased expenditure on food as well as other essentials. Manley, Gitter, and Slavchevska (2013) provide a detailed review of a large number of evaluations of various cash transfer programmes. The general finding of most studies is that programmes that involve substantial transfers result in higher food consumption and improved dietary quality. Beneficiary households consume more fruit, vegetables, and animal-source foods than households with similar economic status who are not covered by cash transfer programmes. Expenditure on food accounts for the bulk of the money provided by cash transfer programmes in developing countries. Cash transfer programmes that provide substantial transfers and are accompanied by other interventions providing access to nutritionally rich food items are associated with improved nutritional outcomes. Food coupons, when substantial in their real value, have been found to significantly contribute to improving dietary diversity (Hidrobo et al., 2014). On the other hand, when the real value of transfers is very small, benefits in terms of increased consumption and improved nutritional outcomes are not significant.

In comparison with programmes that entitle beneficiaries to a certain amount of food, an important limitation of cash transfer programmes is that the entitlements for beneficiaries are not protected against inflation. Very few cash transfers have entitlements indexed to inflation. There are many examples in low-income countries where cash transfer and food stamps programmes became insignificant because of depreciation of the real value of transfers, and the unwillingness of governments and donors to index entitlements against inflation.

Rapid devaluation in the value of food stamps because of food price inflation is the most serious problem that food stamp programmes in developing countries have faced (Swaminathan, 2004). Sri Lanka, where the food stamps programme started in 1978, is one of the few developing countries that continues to have a food stamps programme. However, as shown by Edirisinghe (1987), the real value of food stamps in Sri Lanka fell to about half their original value within three years of introduction. A careful assessment of the shift from a universal food subsidy scheme to food stamps in Sri Lanka by Anand and Kanbur (1991) found that "the burden of real cuts in the food subsidy budget is likely to have fallen disproportionately on the poor". With the low value of transfers involved, food stamps in Sri Lanka have not had any significant impact on nutritional outcomes. In Jamaica, another country where a food stamps programme has been implemented for a long time, devaluation of the real value of food stamps has marginalized the significance of the programme.

Sabates-Wheeler and Devereux (2010) reviewed the impact of food price crisis on the real value of cash entitlements under the Productive Safety Net Programme (PSNP) in Ethiopia. Under different conditions, participating households under the PSNP are provided food or cash, employment in public works, as well as other specified goods and services. They show that the real value of cash transfers in terms of staple cereals varied considerably across districts and seasons because of variations in prices; the real value of cash transfers in terms of staple cereals had eroded to less than half within just four years since the inception of the PSNP.

Sabates-Wheeler and Devereux (2010) highlight that not only has the real value of cash transfers diminished because of food price inflation, in places where food supply is constrained and entirely dependent on unregulated private traders, cash transfer itself can exacerbate inflation. This in turn further diminishes purchasing power and particularly adversely affects vulnerable households that are excluded from the cash transfer programmes. Cunha, De Giorgi, and Jayachandran (2011) studied the inflationary impact of cash and food provisioning using data from benefi-ciaries of the Mexican Programa de Apoyo Alimentario (PAL), which allows beneficiaries to choose between cash and in-kind transfers. In half of the villages studied, poor households were directly provided food through the PAL; in 25 percent of the villages, beneficiary households were provided equivalent amounts in cash; while in the remaining control villages, no transfers were provided. The study found that food provisioning contributed to bringing down inflation by increasing supply along with increasing demand for food, while cash transfer programmes exacerbated inflation. This difference alone accounted for an 11 percent additional benefit from food provisioning against cash transfers.

Since beneficiaries of cash transfers/food coupons purchase food from the market, governments are not required to procure, stock, and distribute food. Cash transfers/food coupons can be used when infrastructure for public procurement, supply-chain management, and distribution does not exist for running food distribution programmes. In countries where food distribution programmes only provide staple grain, cash transfers (in particular, food coupons) can be used as a complement to improve access to perishable commodities like fruit, vegetables, and milk.

However, the flip side of this aspect of cash transfers/food coupon programmes is that governments do not intervene on the supply-side to ensure that adequate food is available to meet the demands of the programmes. Without such an intervention, the impact of a food coupon/cash transfer programme on production is mediated by the market, and may not be optimal for long-term food security, nutritional outcomes or sustainability. Besides, as discussed already, imperfections in the functioning of markets and supply-side bottlenecks can create serious inflationary imbalances.

It is widely recognized that the use of conditionalities requires considerable supply side investments to ensure availability of services upon which provision of cash is made conditional (Fernald, 2013; Ghosh, 2011). Some conditional cash transfers have been criticized for large-scale exclusion of particularly vulnerable sections of the population because of their inability to meet conditions (Garcia and Moore, 2012). Also, the cost of imposing and monitoring conditionalities can be high, and may outweigh the benefits of imposing them. In Sub-Saharan Africa, most cash transfer programmes are either unconditional or have soft conditionalities not requiring mandatory compliance as supply constraints and the inability of many beneficiaries to comply with the conditionalities could result in large-scale exclusion of many of the poorest and most vulnerable (Garcia and Moore, 2012). In Mexico, the Programa de Apoyo Alimentario (PAL) was started in 2003 to provide support to communities whose households are unable to participate in Oportunidades because of absence of a school or health clinic nearby. Conditionalities under the PAL are softer than in Oportunidades, and are not strictly enforced.

There can also be considerable leakage and fraud in cash transfer programmes; preventing them usually entails considerable monitoring costs. Where penetration of formal financial systems is low, regulatory systems are weak, and corruption in the public services is serious, cash distribution can create significant opportunities for fraud at different stages of programme implementation. Ellis, Devereux, and White (2009) have documented various kinds of problems in targeting social protection programmes in Africa. For example, in Lesotho's Old Age Pension programme, 'ghost beneficiaries' were created to secure benefits. In various programmes in many countries, headmen, officials, and other powerful people have cornered substantial benefits. The experience with cash transfers in India's Integrated Rural Development Programme (IRDP) in the 1980s was similar. Given the attractiveness of cash hand-outs, implementation of the programme was marred by elite capture, leakages, and corruption (see, among others, Drèze, 1990; Guhan, 1980; Rath, 1985; Shankar, 1991). In India, recent programmes involving cash payments have also faced the problem of significant leakages (see, for example, Mann and Pande, 2012; Shankar and Gaiha, 2013; Usami and Rawal, 2012).

Dealing with under-5 child and maternal nutrition deficiencies

It is now well recognized that preventing stunting and other forms of severe undernutrition requires special attention to nutrition deficiencies afflicting mothers and children under 5 years of age. Recent studies suggest that the first thousand days from conception until reaching the age of 2 are the most important for long-term human development. Inadequate nutrition during this period is the most important cause of long-term undernutrition. Securing improvements in the nutrition of pregnant and lactating women, infants and young children requires that specific nutrition programmes be linked with general social protection programmes, as well as programmes for improving access to safe water, sanitation, and health care.

Access to nutritious food for mothers and children under 5 can be improved by community child-care facilities as well as other social protection policies. Statistical evidence from various conditional cash transfer programmes in Latin America shows significant improvements in the nutritional status of infants and young children when social protection programmes are linked with nutritional programmes. For example, evaluations of Mexico's Oportunidades show an increase of about 1 cm in height among children from beneficiary households compared to controls, and an increase of 0.13 kg in birth weight among children born in beneficiary households compared to controls. Various studies have found improvements in the Z-scores of height-for-age of children from beneficiary households of various social protection programmes, in comparison with controls (WHO, 2013). Improvements in the access of pregnant women from beneficiary households to antenatal care have also been noted (UNICEF, 2008).

The WHO's comparison of improvements in child nutrition in different programmes across the world with the programme intensity – measured in terms of the number of community health and nutrition workers (CHNWs) deployed – found that the extent of contact between trained community workers and mothers with children is crucial. Programmes with more than 30 CHNWs per 1,000 children achieved 1–2 percentage points per year reduction in prevalence of underweight. However, owing to considerable variation in the way resources are used, no clear relationship could be seen between the amount of resources provided under nutrition programmes and outcomes (WHO, 2013).

It is important to note that not all nutrition programmes have significantly impacted maternal and child nutrition. For example, studies of India's Integrated Child Development Services (ICDS) have found little or no impact on child undernutrition (Lokshin *et al.*, 2005).

An important lesson to draw from the experience of implementing nutrition programmes is that when nutrition programmes work in isolation, without utilizing synergies with social protection programmes and programmes for improving access to safe water, sanitation, and health care, the impacts are limited. On the other hand, synergies among various programmes ensure significant gains in nutritional outcomes of infants and young children.

Coverage of social protection programmes

Social protection is most effective when designed to provide basic universal coverage. Providing basic social protection coverage to everyone is also important from a human rights-based perspective. Universal social protection programmes need to be combined with specific interventions targeted at nutritionally vulnerable populations, such as children, as well as pregnant and lactating women.

The coverage of social security systems has been narrowed and public spending on social security cut by the structural adjustment programmes implemented in developing countries across the world from the 1980s. As part of the conditions of these programmes, leading international finance institutions argued to minimize social provisioning. Instead, social safety nets, narrowly targeted at the poorest and most vulnerable, were introduced from the 1990s for the purpose of providing security against shocks (Holzmann, Sherburne-Benz, and Tesliuc, 2003; Mkandawire, 2005).

It has long been recognized that means-tested targeting entails considerable costs. Sen (1995) argues that targeting involves significant direct and indirect costs. Targeting subsidies can affect economic behaviour, stigmatize beneficiaries, involve considerable administrative costs, and be invasive by requiring extensive disclosures to become eligible for benefits.

He argues that programmes targeted narrowly at the very poor are difficult to sustain politically because the beneficiaries are likely to have limited political clout. On the other hand, programmes that provide a universal minimum entitlement are likely to find much greater political support.

In a detailed review of targeting in social protection programmes, Mkandawire (2005) identifies three major problems. First, given the limited capacity of governments in poor countries and the predominance of informal economic relations, targeting based on assessment of incomes and means is necessarily imprecise, involving very high administrative costs, and inviting problems of corruption, theft, and fraud.[3] Other, more blunt forms of targeting involve more likely errors of both wrongful exclusion and wrongful inclusion. Given serious asymmetries of information, targeting produced "perverse incentives" and was "an open invitation to rent seeking and corruption". Secondly, targeting creates serious political problems. These arise from overall reductions in budgets, the stigmatizing effects of targeting, the invasiveness of measurement for targeting purposes, and the compounding "paternalistic and clientelistic practices of bureaucracies". Thirdly, targeting creates a disincentive for beneficiaries to achieve outcomes that would disqualify them from receiving benefits. Ellis (2012) argues that, with the high prevalence of poverty and vulnerability, narrowly targeted cash transfers that privilege a few of the many poor and vulnerable are socially divisive.

It is common to assess targeting in terms of errors of wrongful exclusion of the eligible (Type I errors) and wrongful inclusion of those not eligible (Type II errors). One of the most detailed and careful studies of errors in targeting by Cornia and Stewart (1993) concluded that replacement of universal schemes by targeted schemes in a number of countries has been associated with a major increase in errors of wrongful exclusion, with some reduction in errors of wrongful inclusion. Large-scale exclusion of those eligible has been a feature of most narrowly targeted social protection programmes. For example, Ellis, Devereux, and White (2009) estimated that 83 percent of poor aged persons were excluded from the Food Subsidy Programme in Mozambique that provides targeted cash transfers to the old, people with disabilities, and the chronically ill among the poor. Several studies of targeting in Asia have also reported large errors of exclusion and leakages (see, for example, Swaminathan, 2000; Swaminathan and Misra, 2001; and Weiss, 2005)

---

[3] In a review of targeted programmes, Coady, Grosh, and Hoddinott (2004) observe that "in most cases it appears that corruption and theft contribute more to total program expenses than legitimate administrative expenses". Various contributions in Weiss (2005) record serious problems of corruption and malpractices in targeted programmes in Asia.

Box 3.3 ICN2 Framework for Action: Recommended actions on social protection

The ICN2 Framework for Action calls for incorporation of nutrition objectives into social protection programmes, and use of cash and food transfers to ensure that people have access to nutritionally adequate food, and to take action to improve incomes of the vulnerable population through decent jobs and improved prospects of self-employment.

- Recommendation 22: Incorporate nutrition objectives into social protection programmes and into humanitarian assistance safety net programmes.

- Recommendation 23: Use cash and food transfers, including school feeding programmes and other forms of social protection for vulnerable populations to improve diets through better access to food which conforms with the beliefs, culture, traditions, dietary habits and preferences of individuals in accordance with national and international laws and obligations, and which is nutritionally adequate for healthy diets.

- Recommendation 24: Increase income for the most vulnerable populations by creating decent jobs for all, including through the promotion of self-employment.

Evidence from three decades of implementation of targeted anti-poverty and social protection schemes in the developing countries shows that the combination of narrow targeting and reduced benefits can render social protection ineffective in countries where deprivation is widespread and poverty high. In view of this, a consensus is emerging that it is best to have broad-based or universal coverage of social protection that provides rights-based guarantees to a nationally determined minimum set of goods and services. Endorsing the idea of a universal social protection floor, the High Level Panel of Eminent Persons on the Post-2015 Development Agenda convened by the United Nations Secretary-General called for "leaving no-one behind".

Synergies among different types of interventions

When social protection programmes are integrated with rural or agricultural development policies and nutrition initiatives, the synergies have strong multiplier effects. Social protection measures are key to protect the poor from hunger and food insecurity, especially when decent employment growth has been sluggish. When integrated with rural and agricultural development policies as well as special nutrition initiatives, impressive results follow.

Countries should implement programmes for a nationally determined basic social protection floor, and strive to ensure that such programmes cover everyone and can provide those in need with adequate nutritious food. Where such programmes have been implemented, even modest public expenditures have been found to have significant positive impacts on investment, productivity, and incomes. Integrating social protection programmes with programmes for agricultural development can maximize the impact on incomes and productivity, particularly of small-scale producers. Integration of nutrition programmes with social protection programmes is crucial for ensuring that special nutritional support for women, infants, and young children translates into positive nutritional outcomes.

4

Role of Fortification and Supplementation

Nutrition is complex and multidimensional. While there has not been a consensus on a broad-based plan to tackle malnutrition across the world, the problems are better understood now, with options for addressing malnutrition increasingly well known. The underlying cause of micronutrient deficiencies is the poor quality of diet, lacking sufficient nutrient-dense animal-source foods, fruit, and vegetables. Food-based approaches – which focus on ensuring that the diets of people include diverse, nutritionally rich foods – provide sustainable long-term solutions for controlling and overcoming micronutrient deficiencies.

In addition to improving the composition of diets, enhancement of the nutrient content of staple food through chemical and agronomic fortification is known to be a cost-effective and complementary means to deliver specific nutrients such as iron, zinc, and vitamins. Fortification has been used across many countries through most of the twentieth century.

More recently, two other approaches have been advocated to tackle micronutrient deficiencies: genetic biofortification and supplementation. Genetic biofortification refers to breeding varieties and hybrids rich in specific nutrients, and introducing these nutrient-rich foods into people's diets. Supplementation refers to the direct intake of micronutrients, usually in the form of tablets/capsules. Of late it has been argued – most importantly, in the June 2013 issue of the Maternal and Child Nutrition Series of the British Medical Association's influential journal, *The Lancet* – that nutritional supplements provide a rapid and cost-effective means of dealing with the widespread problem of malnutrition.

What part can fortification – chemical, agronomic, and genetic – play in ending malnutrition? Can ending malnutrition be led by supplementation? This chapter examines the evidence to seek answers to these questions.

Chemical fortification of food

Large-scale fortification has been used since the early twentieth century to deal with micronutrient deficiencies. Before discussing the experiences with fortification and their potential, it is important to distinguish between regulated fortification as part of public initiatives to deal with specific nutritional deficiencies, and unregulated commercial uses of fortification, often to claim health benefits from otherwise not-so healthy and energy-dense foods. The discussion here specifically deals with the potential of regulated fortification in dealing with the problem of micronutrient deficiencies.

In general, fortification has been effectively deployed in conditions where

- a specific micronutrient deficiency is widespread in the population;

- the desired micronutrient requirement is more or less uniform across different sections of the population;

- specific agro-ecological limitations make it difficult to meet micronutrient requirements through food systems, at least in the short run; and

- desired micronutrients can be provided along with a widely consumed component of the diet without adverse implications of adding the micronutrient to the item.

Fortification has often been made mandatory to ensure widespread adoption of micronutrient-fortified food. In many countries across the world, governments have made iodization of salt mandatory (see Box 4.1). Similarly, in many countries, vitamin A fortification of sugar and iron fortification of wheat flour have been made mandatory.

Fortification is best done through food items regularly consumed by most of the population. Salt, sugar, cereals, edible oils, and milk have been commonly used as fortification carriers. There are several technical aspects that determine the choice of carrier and the fortificant used to deal with a particular micronutrient deficiency. Bio-availability and absorption of a micronutrient depend on the fortificant and carrier used. For example, absorption of iron from ferrous sulphate, the most common fortificant used for iron, is negatively related to the bran content of flour as bran inhibits the absorption of iron. In the case of iodine, iodine is lost to the atmosphere in the event of exposure to moisture, heat, and sunlight. Potassium iodate is known to be a more stable fortificant than potassium iodide and sodium iodide. The stability of iodized salt can also be improved by the use of stabilizers and good packaging (Biber, Unak, and Yurt, 2002; Diosady *et al.*, 1998; Kelly, 1953). Some fortificants affect the physical properties of food, like taste and colour, and thus may not be readily accepted by target populations. In the 1970s, Guatemala introduced sugar fortified with NaFeEDTA. However, NaFeEDTA changed the colour of foods and beverages to which the fortified sugar was added, resulting in its poor acceptability. The introduction of colour-neutral iron fortificants in Brazil, on the other hand, has been much more successful (Beinner and Lamounier, 2003; Pineda, 1998). There are also significant differences in the costs of different fortificants (Allen *et al.*, 2006).

Fortification has been most successful in addressing iodine and vitamin A deficiencies. Iron, folate, and zinc fortifications have also been widely used; although the success of such programmes has been mixed.

A review of the literature on fortification programmes across the world suggests that fortification is most successful where the cost of fortification is a relatively small share of the total cost of the product. Darnton-Hill *et al.* (1999) point out that the fortification of wheat flour in Latin America added less than 0.5 percent to the retail price of flour. The high costs of fortification make it commercially less attractive as fortified foods cannot be priced much higher than unfortified products (Bressani, 2000; Darnton-Hill *et al.*, 1999; Hertrampf, 2002).

Fortification has been most successful where the food item being fortified is produced on a large scale by a few private or public producers (Bressani, 2000). In countries where local small-scale grain milling is common, fortification is more difficult to implement and regulate. Implementation of vitamin A fortification of sugar in many Latin American countries and salt iodization in many countries across the world has been feasible because sugar and salt are mainly manufactured in the organized sector. On the other hand, the impact of iron and folate fortification of flour on the prevalence of iron-deficiency anaemia has been mixed. In most Latin American countries, wheat milling is highly centralized, large scale, and in the organized sector. Most of these countries have made wheat fortification mandatory. This has been implemented relatively effectively because of the organized nature of wheat milling (Bressani, 2000; Darnton-Hill *et al.*, 1999). On the other hand, iron fortification of maize flour has been limited, not only for technical reasons, but also because the milling of maize, in particular wet milling, is much more decentralized and small-scale than wheat milling. Traditionally, maize is used in Latin America after nixtamalization, which involves boiling and soaking maize with lime before grinding it wet into a dough. The process has been industrialized to a significant degree through introduction of nixtamalized corn flour as a substitute for wet-ground corn (maize) dough. This has opened the possibilities of iron fortification of maize flour in Latin America (Bressani, Rooney, and Salvidar, 1997).

Box 4.1 Eradicating Iodine Deficiency through Mandatory Iodine Fortification of Salt

---

Iodine deficiency causes diseases like goitre and nodular hyperthyroidism, and results in reduced productivity. It leads to cognitive impairment among children. Iodine-deficient pregnant women face a higher risk of abortion, a higher probability of having babies with low birth weight and a higher probability of infant mortality (Speeckaert *et al.*, 2011). In 1990, the World Health Assembly accepted the elimination of iodine deficiency as a public health goal for all countries.

Various supplementation and fortification methods have been implemented across the world to deal with iodine deficiency. In 1994, a UNICEF–WHO Joint Committee endorsed iodized salt as a safe and effective strategy for ensuring sufficient intake of iodine by all persons.

The process of iodization is simple and cost-effective, and does not alter the taste, odour, and colour of salt. Given that salt is universally consumed, it is considered an excellent vehicle for iodine.

Health policies mandating iodization of salt have seen remarkable progress in improving iodine status and reducing the prevalence of goitre and cretinism in countries with severe iodine deficiencies. In South Africa, iodization of salt has resulted in the near-eradication of iodine deficiency in schoolchildren after one year of implementation (Jooste, Weight, and Lombard, 2000). The long-term supply of iodized salt in regions of Pakistan where goitre is endemic resulted in significant decreases in its prevalence. The proportion of severely iodine deficient households was reduced to a marginal level with constant monitoring and adjustment in iodine supplementation levels (Ali *et al.*, 1992). Essentially, periodic monitoring of iodine status in women and children is imperative to ensure the efficacy of iodine fortification. The Swiss population witnessed dramatic reduction in the prevalence of goitre with the consumption of iodized salt (Allen *et al.*, 2006). Regular monitoring helped the government in Switzerland to achieve sufficient iodine nutrition in women and children by changing the concentration of iodine in salt in response to the changing dietary habits of the population (Zimmermann *et al.*, 2005).

As iron deficiency reduces the efficacy of iodine fortification (Allen *et al.*, 2006), some countries have used double fortification of salt with iodine and iron. A review of evidence suggests that while double fortification improves the absorption of iodine, it diminishes the stability of iodine in salt, and the iron intake through salt only partially covers iron requirements (Baxter and Zlotkin, 2015).

There are three main concerns with the use of iodized salt as the main means for dealing with iodine deficiency. First, iodine has limited stability and tends to dissipate over time because of exposure to moisture, light, and heat. Good packaging and storage, which improve stability considerably, remain a problem in developing countries and at the household level.

Secondly, strong evidence links high salt intake to hypertension and other cardiovascular problems (WHO, 2012). A WHO–FAO Joint Expert Consultation recommended that salt intake be reduced to 5 grams per day per person (WHO/FAO, 2003). Unless the concentration of iodine in salt is adequately increased, reduced salt intake would reduce intake of iodine. A decline in iodine intake and reappearance of iodine deficiency have already been noticed in some developed countries on account of inadequate intake of iodine (Renner, 2010). However, increasing the concentration of iodine reduces its stability, making it difficult to use salt as the main vehicle for the delivery of iodine. Further research is required to develop technology to increase the concentration of iodine in salt without adversely affecting iodine stability and other properties, and to find other suitable carriers for iodine.

Finally, salt fortification becomes difficult to implement and monitor where salt production is decentralized. This is important, for example, in coastal areas, where sea salt is locally produced. Rasheed *et al.* (2001) have shown that only 2 percent of households consumed iodized salt in the coastal regions of Bangladesh. The easy availability of untreated salt at lower cost and lack of awareness of the health effects of iodized salt are the main factors that limit the use of iodized salt in the coastal areas of Bangladesh.

FIGURE 4.1 Proportion of households consuming adequately iodized salt, by country, 2000–13

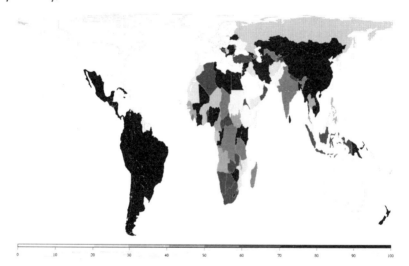

In all, it is estimated that about 75 percent of households worldwide use adequately iodized salt. Among the regions, East Asia and the Pacific has the highest proportion – 87 percent – of households consuming adequately iodized salt, close to the global target of 90 percent salt iodization. In all, 69 countries reached the target of 90 percent coverage of salt iodization by 2011 (UNICEF, 2013 and Figure 4.1). While commendable, it is critical to maintain the momentum to ensure iodized salt for the remaining population of the world. Universal use of adequately iodized salt requires research coordination for technical improvements, introduction of mandatory provisions, expanding awareness-raising, as well as careful regulation and monitoring at the national level to overcome administrative, social, medical, and other barriers to eradicating iodine deficiency.

On the other hand, in many Asian and African countries with large rural populations, a substantial part of the food consumed by households is home-produced, and grain milling is decentralized and on a small scale. These make implementation and regulation of fortification more difficult, and its reach across the target population more limited. Although there have been some experiments in distributing pre-mixed nutrients for home fortification, in most of these countries, fortified flour constitutes a relatively small share of total consumption.

Although the fortification of salt and sugar has been relatively successful in many countries, an important concern is that the promotion of fortified salt and sugar could work against attempts to reduce salt and sugar intake by the population. It is, therefore, recommended that promotion of iodized salt and programmes for reducing salt intake should closely collaborate to ensure that promotion of the use of iodized salt does not result in public promotion of salt intake (WHO, 2008). Some writings on iron fortification have advocated the use of soft drinks as a vehicle for iron fortification to deal with iron-deficiency anaemia among children and women (Layrisse *et al.*, 1976; Wojcicki and Heyman, 2010). Such arguments ignore the serious dietary imbalances and public health problems caused by increasing the intake of sugar-dense beverages. Promoting sugar-dense beverages as a vehicle for dealing with iron-deficiency anaemia carries a serious risk of inducing excess sugar consumption.

Fortification is a cost-effective method of enriching diets to deal with specific deficiencies. Fortification may be particularly useful in the short run for populations that buy centrally processed foods. There are, however, limitations of fortification in reaching rural consumers for whom much of the basic diet is produced at home. When micronutrient requirements vary across the population (say, between men, women, and children), fortification can only be used to meet the minimal requirement, and may have to be combined with additional interventions for groups that need additional intake of micronutrients.

Agronomic biofortification

Another approach to augment the nutrient content of food is through fortification at the stage of crop production itself. This can be done either through application of nutrients along with fertilizers or irrigation water, or by developing crop varieties and hybrids that are rich in a particular nutrient.

Deficiencies of micronutrients, for example, zinc and iodine, can be traced in many countries to the depletion of these nutrients in the soil. Fortification through soil enrichment is known to be an effective way of dealing with zinc, iodine, and selenium deficiencies (Alloway, 2009; Cakmak, 2008, 2009; Rengel, Batten, and Crowley, 1999).

In the Central Anatolia region of Turkey, fertilizers enriched with zinc were used for cultivation of zinc-absorbent wheat varieties (Cakmak *et al.*, 1999). It has been argued that zinc enrichment of fertilizers can go a long way in dealing with zinc deficiencies in India, where about half the soils are deficient in zinc (Cakmak, 2009). Hence, the Government of India has introduced additional subsidies to fertilizer manufacturers for zinc fortification of fertilizers, and to farmers for using zinc fertilizers (Das and Green, 2013).

In China, potassium iodate was added to canal irrigation water to enrich the soils with iodine (Cao *et al.*, 1994). The empirical evidence showed that the iodination of canal water significantly reduced iodine deficiency among pregnant women, which in turn resulted in a significant drop in infant and neonatal mortality (DeLong *et al.*, 1997).

Since the mid-1980s, sodium selenate has been used to enrich fertilizers in Finland. This is known to have helped improve selenium intake in Finland (Aro, Alfthan, and Varo, 1995; Varo *et al.*, 1988).

Fortification through soil enrichment is particularly useful where the consumption of staple grains for a large proportion of households is based on home production. In such cases, the fortification of flour at the stage of milling may not be effective. Agronomic fortification is effective and can be introduced relatively quickly without major new investments in research and extension.

Genetic biofortification

More recently, genetic biofortification, which involves enhancing the nutrition content of crops through breeding, has been promoted as a new approach to fortification, and is increasingly seen as an alternative, effective means of delivering specific micronutrients along with food. A lot of work has been done on biofortification by HarvestPlus, a CGIAR (Consultative Group for International Agricultural Research) programme.[1]

Golden Rice, a variety of rice enriched with vitamin A, is the most well-known case of a biofortified crop. Proponents of Golden Rice argue that it has the potential to be a complementary source of vitamin A, and could be a cost-effective means of reducing vitamin A deficiency (Dawe, Robertson, and Unnevehr, 2002; Stein, Sachdev, and Qaim, 2008). On the other hand, critics have argued that the levels of β-Carotene in Golden Rice are too low and do not make sufficient contribution to vitamin A requirements (Grusak, 2005). There are also economic issues involved in the adoption of Golden Rice. Its cost-effectiveness depends on its widespread adoption across Asia.

---

[1] For further details, see Bouis (1999, 2000), Carvalho and Vasconcelos (2013), HarvestPlus (2014), Mayer, Pfeiffer, and Beyer (2008), Meenakshi *et al.* (2010), Saltzman *et al.* (2013), Smith (2013), and Stein *et al.* (2008), and www.harvestplus.org.

But a single seed strain is not going to be suitable for the diverse agro-ecological conditions in which rice is produced across Asia.

Golden Rice has met with great resistance from research and civil society groups opposed to genetically modified seeds. Very few Asian countries have legal frameworks in place for testing and introduction of transgenic food crops. This has resulted in long delays in the widespread adoption of Golden Rice even to deal with vitamin A deficiencies.

While Golden Rice has faced obstacles due to being a genetically modified crop, several other biofortified crops have been developed through conventional open pollination and other plant-breeding methods. Some of these have already been released for production while many others are at different stages of development. Rich in β-Carotene, the Orange Sweet Potato has been successfully introduced in Mozambique and Uganda to deal with vitamin A deficiencies. Biofortified Orange Sweet Potato accounts for about 56 percent of the area cultivated with sweet potato in Mozambique, and about 44 percent of the area cultivated with sweet potato in Uganda. HarvestPlus, International Crops Research Institute for the Semi-Arid Tropics, various agricultural universities in India, and seed companies are partnering to produce crossbreeds of high-yielding pearlt millet that are rich in iron and zinc. A variety rich in iron, ICTP 8203-Fe, was released in India in 2013, and is being tested in Niger. In Bangladesh, sweet potato, tomato, pumpkin, mango, and guava enriched with vitamin A have been developed. The Bangladesh Rice Research Institute has developed rice varieties biofortified with zinc, which have already been released for production by farmers.[2] In March 2015, the Pakistan Agriculture Research Council released zinc-fortified varieties of wheat developed in collaboration with HarvestPlus.[3]

There is no independent research yet on the impact of the adoption of biofortified crops on nutritional outcomes of the population at large. A few studies, all done with the support of agencies involved in the development of biofortified crops, have shown that introduction of β-Carotene-rich Orange Sweet Potato in Mozambique and Uganda has lowered the prevalence of vitamin A deficiency among children and women who consumed the biofortified produce (Hotz et al., 2012a, 2012b). More research and evidence are needed to assess the cost-effectiveness, acceptability, and impact of biofortified crops on the overall nutrition of populations. The incorporation of biofortified crops in the agricultural and nutrition strategies of countries will require addressing several policy issues relating to the ownership and control of the technology, the cost of seeds to farmers, cost at which other complementary inputs (like fertilizers, pesticides, and water) needed for

---

[2] www.harvestplus.org/sites/default/files/Bangladesh%20Statement%20at%20ICN2.pdf.
[3] www.dawn.com/news/1167202.

crop production are made available to farmers, their suitability to the agro-ecological context, and the nutritional outcomes of their adoption.

Supplementation

The June 2013 issue of *The Lancet*, as part of its Maternal and Child Nutrition Series, argued that nutritional supplements provide a rapid and cost-effective means of dealing with micronutrient deficiencies.[4] In the issue, Bhutta *et al.* (2013) argued that, unlike conventional strategies based on breastfeeding and provision of nutritious foods through lunch or noon-meal schemes and other social protection programmes targeting pregnant women, lactating women, and children, considerable evidence based on randomized control trials show the benefits of supplements in reducing the incidence of stunting. Their detailed analysis of quantitative evidence on the effects of supplements on nutritional outcomes suggested that a total investment of US$ 9.6 billion on ten nutrition-related interventions in thirty-four focus countries would reduce mortality among children aged less than 5 years by about 15 percent. This finding was used to make the argument that a supplementation-based strategy to deal with maternal and child malnutrition is promisingly cost-effective.

While supplementation-led interventions may be appropriate in some contexts, especially in the short term, or in the face of emergencies such as conflicts or natural disasters, exclusive focus on micronutrient supplementation distracts from addressing the deeper causes of malnutrition, and undermines the development of sustainable long-term solutions to micronutrient deficiencies. The case for a supplement-led strategy for dealing with micronutrient deficiencies is problematic on various grounds.

As pointed out by Pinstrup-Andersen (2013) in a comment on Maternal and Child Nutrition series papers in *The Lancet*, the fixation on randomized control trials as the only legitimate evidence is misplaced as it is impossible to apply such methods to testing food systems.

An exclusive focus on micronutrient supplementation without addressing the fundamental causes of malnutrition, particularly those related to the food system, can be extremely problematic and render nutrition policies ineffective. In most cases, micronutrient supplementation cannot be very effective without adequate food. Providing micronutrients without adequate food can even have negative effects.

Also, while the beneficial effects of some forms of supplementation – for example, iron supplementation among pregnant women – are well established, the evidence is much less clear in many cases. For example, the efficacy of maternal and neonatal vitamin A supplementation has been

---

[4] www.thelancet.com/series/maternal-and-child-nutrition.

questioned, and the recent recommendations for inclusion of early neonatal vitamin A supplementation in nutrition programmes have been severely criticized.[5]

Additionally, focusing on supplements often favours reliance on and involvement of the biochemical and pharmaceutical industries, which would develop a vested interest in discouraging alternative long-term options for addressing malnutrition on a more affordable and sustainable basis. If the supplements are produced domestically – which may be better for the national economy – time and resources will be needed to establish local manufacturing systems, distribution systems, and regulatory structures. However, such efforts to develop national capacities are likely to be thwarted by international trade, investment, and intellectual property rights agreements and regulations driven by powerful corporate lobbies.

In view of these problems, the role of supplements is best limited to dealing with specific, short-term requirements such as providing iron and folic acid supplements during the period of pregnancy.

Ending malnutrition: Diet-based or supplementation-led?

In the recent policy literature on nutrition, a distinction is often made between nutrition-specific interventions and nutrition-sensitive interventions. Nutrition-specific interventions are based on different forms of supplementation. Addressing specific forms of malnutrition is their primary objective. Nutrition-sensitive interventions, on the other hand, are multisectoral interventions with varied primary objectives – for example, alleviation of poverty, development of agriculture, improving educational attainments, or improving access to water, sanitation, and health facilities – that are designed so as to result in improved nutrition as a side effect.

UNICEF (1990) developed a conceptual framework on causes of malnutrition in 1990. The framework identified the basic causes (the socio-economic and political contexts), underlying causes (food insecurity, inadequate health care, unhealthy household environment), and immediate causes (inadequate dietary intake and diseases) of malnutrition, and was used to develop UNICEF's multisectoral strategy on malnutrition among women and children. This was one of the first attempts to conceptualize multisectoral linkages of nutrition, and has been adapted and widely used to guide the nutrition strategies of many agencies worldwide (see chapter 6).

More recently, the Scaling Up Nutrition (SUN) movement's Framework for Action paper called for combining the scaling up of nutrition-specific interventions with broader multisectoral approaches (SUN, 2009). This approach has been widely accepted by many international agencies as well

---

[5] See, for example, Haider and Bhutta (2015) and Mason *et al.* (2015).

as countries. The World Bank's paper on multisectoral approaches towards nutrition builds upon the SUN Framework for Action to develop guidelines for making the World Bank's interventions in various sectors nutrition-sensitive (Alderman *et al.*, 2013). USAID's 2014 Multisectoral Nutrition Strategy identifies scaling up "effective, integrated nutrition-specific and -sensitive interventions, programs, and systems across humanitarian and development contexts" as its strategic objective (USAID, 2014). DFID's position paper on undernutrition talks of a two-pronged strategy to deal with child stunting: first, scaling up nutrition specific interventions, and second, to use nutrition-sensitive interventions to deal with residual child stunting that cannot be eradicated merely by nutrition-specific interventions (DFID, 2011).

Although recognizing the complementary role of nutrition-sensitive multisectoral interventions, most of these recent approaches give primacy to nutrition-specific interventions. Concrete, actionable strategies with precise estimates of costs are presented for nutrition-specific interventions. On the other hand, nutrition-sensitive interventions in other areas, including in food systems, are presented as complementary strategies, typically without specific budgetary commitments. This misplaced emphasis on supplementation needs to be corrected.

It is important that nutrition strategies are based on the centrality of food systems in providing nutrition. Good nutrition requires, first and foremost, ensuring availability of and access to more diverse diets and nutritious foods. In most cases, micronutrients can be delivered cost-effectively and sustainably through diverse and adequately nutritious diets. This requires that food systems are developed to make available a diverse variety of foods; that social protection systems are put in place to ensure everyone has access to adequate and nutritious foods; that access to safe water, and improved sanitation and basic health care, are available for all.

Where necessary, and where cost-effective technologies are easily available, the nutrient content of food may be enhanced through fortification. Certain types of regulated fortification – salt iodization, for example – are an essential component of the strategy to make food systems nutrition-sensitive. Regulated fortification can be used for specific problems such as iodine deficiency, for which solutions are easily available and impacts well established. Greater evidence is needed to assess the cost implications, efficacy and impact of new approaches like genetic biofortification.

Supplementation may also be necessary at times as an urgent short-term solution when specific categories of people (for example, pregnant women and infants) are severely nutrient-deficient and immediate interventions are needed. Some micronutrients, such as iron and folic acid, are commonly delivered to pregnant women through supplements in both rich and poor countries. Supplementation can be used selectively in such contexts, though these have to be accompanied with simultaneous interventions to ensure adequate food intake.

Box 4.2 ICN2 Framework for Action: Selective use of fortification and supplementation

The ICN2 Framework for Action provides a useful guide in this respect. With a clear focus on developing "sustainable food systems promoting healthy diets", the Framework for Action suggests selective use of fortification and supplementation for dealing with anaemia among pregnant and menstruating women and young children, and zinc supplementation to prevent diarrhoea among children.

Recommended actions to address anaemia in women of reproductive age

- Recommendation 42: Improve intake of micronutrients through consumption of nutrient-dense foods, especially foods rich in iron, where necessary, through fortification and supplementation strategies, and promote healthy and diversified diets.

- Recommendation 43: Provide daily iron and folic acid and other micronutrient supplementation to pregnant women as part of antenatal care; and intermittent iron and folic acid supplementation to menstruating women where the prevalence of anaemia is 20% or higher, and deworming, where appropriate.

Recommended actions in the health services to improve nutrition

- Recommendation 47: Provide zinc supplementation to reduce the duration and severity of diarrhoea, and to prevent subsequent episodes in children.

- Recommendation 48: Provide iron and, among others, vitamin A supplementation for pre-school children to reduce the risk of anaemia.

5

Improving Access to
Safe Water and Sanitation

Improving access to safe water, sanitation, and basic health services is crucial for the absorption of nutrients that are consumed. Thus it is crucial that efforts to improve diets are combined with improvements in access to safe water, sanitation, and health care. Since issues of access to health care are complex and need to be treated separately, we focus here on outlining the nature of the gaps in access to safe water and sanitation, and the policy priorities for closing these gaps.

Impact of access to safe water and sanitation on malnutrition

Unsafe water and unhygienic sanitation practices result in several infectious diseases, most notably diarrhoea and soil-transmitted helminths (STH, worms). Compounded by the lack of access to basic health services, diarrhoea and STH severely reduce the absorption of nutrients that are consumed. Unsafe water and poor sanitation cause a number of other infectious diseases which increase the need for nutrients and diminish appetites. In the worst situations, malnutrition and diarrhoea can form a vicious cycle as a malnourished person becomes more susceptible to infections and the diseases become more persistent.

There is strong empirical evidence of the adverse impacts of lack of access to safe water and sanitation on health and malnutrition. Pruss-Ustun *et al.* (2004) estimated that, in 2000, unsafe water, sanitation, and hygiene accounted for 1.73 million deaths and 88 percent of the total burden of infectious diarrhoea. In a systematic review of studies of the impact of improvement in access to safe water and sanitation on the morbidity of different diseases, Esrey *et al.* (1991) found that improvement in access to water and sanitation accounted for a median of 26 percent reduction in the incidence of diarrhoea. In a detailed study of eight Sub-Saharan countries, Esrey (1996) found that improvements in access to safe sanitation resulted in taller and heavier children. Interestingly, Esrey (1996) found that improvements in water supply influenced the incidence of diarrhoea and nutritional outcomes only when accompanied by improvements in sanitation and when safe water was available from a source on the household premises. Smith and Haddad (2015), in a detailed econometric assessment of the determinants of decline in child stunting using data for 116 developing countries for a forty-two-year period between 1970 and 2012, found that improvements in access to safe water and sanitation accounted for about 38 percent of the decline in prevalence of child stunting during that period.

Gaps in access to safe water and sanitation

Gaps in safe water supply to household premises and access to improved sanitation are large. Globally, expansion of access to improved sanitation – which often goes hand in hand with expansion of the availability of water on household premises – remains the more widespread problem of the two.

According to the latest statistics available from the WHO–UNICEF Joint Monitoring Programme for Water Supply and Sanitation, for 2012, about 2.5 billion people all over the world did not have access to improved sanitation practices (Table 5.2), while 750 million persons did not have piped water on the premises of their homes (Table 5.1). Expanding access to safe drinking water and improved sanitation has been much more difficult for rural populations. In 2012, over 80 percent of the people who did not have access to safe water supply in their household premises, and over 70 percent of those who did not have access to improved sanitation lived in rural areas.

A total of 325 million persons or over 40 percent of the population of Sub-Saharan Africa did not have access to piped water on their premises. The region is expected to miss the MDG target of halving the proportion of people without access to safe drinking water. About 150 million people in South Asia, 114 million in East Asia, and 67 million in Southeast Asia lacked piped water supply to home premises (Figure 5.1). Of the global population who did not have access to improved sanitation, about 67 percent lived in Asia and about 26 percent in Sub-Saharan Africa (Table 5.2 and Figure 5.2). South Asia, and in particular India, has made very slow progress in expanding sanitation (Box 5.1).

TABLE 5.1 Number of persons and proportion of population not having access to piped water on premises, by region, 2012 (million and percent)

Country	Persons (million)			Prevalence (percent)		
	Urban	Rural	Total	Urban	Rural	Total
East Asia	12	102	114	2	15	8
Southeast Asia	15	51	67	6	15	11
South Asia	25	124	149	4	11	9
Caucasus and Central Asia	1	10	11	4	22	14
West Asia	6	14	20	4	21	9
North Africa	5	8	13	5	11	8
Sub-Saharan Africa	51	274	325	15	48	36
Latin America and Caribbean	14	22	36	3	18	6
Oceania	0	4	5	6	56	44
Developed countries	4	6	9	0	2	1
Total	132	615	748	4	18	11

Source: Based on data from WHO–UNICEF Joint Monitoring Programme for Water Supply and Sanitation.

TABLE 5.2 Number of persons and proportion of population not having access to improved sanitation, by region, 2012 (million and percent)

Country	Persons (million)			Prevalence (percent)		
	Urban	Rural	Total	Urban	Rural	Total
East Asia	190	296	485	24.3	43.4	33.2
Southeast Asia	55	124	179	20	37	29.3
South Asia	205	796	1001	35.9	68.8	58
Oceania	1	6	7	24.3	76.4	64.7
Caucasus and Central Asia	1	2	4	4.1	4.8	4.5
West Asia	6	18	24	4.1	27.3	11.3
North Africa	5	10	14	4.9	13.1	8.5
Sub-Saharan Africa	198	446	644	58.7	77.3	70.4
Latin America and Caribbean	64	46	110	13.2	36.9	18.1
Developed countries	32	22	54	3.3	7.9	4.3
Total	756	1767	2523	20.4	52.8	35.8

Source: Based on data from WHO–UNICEF Joint Monitoring Programme for Water Supply and Sanitation.

FIGURE 5.1 Proportion of population having access to piped water on premises, 2012 (percent)

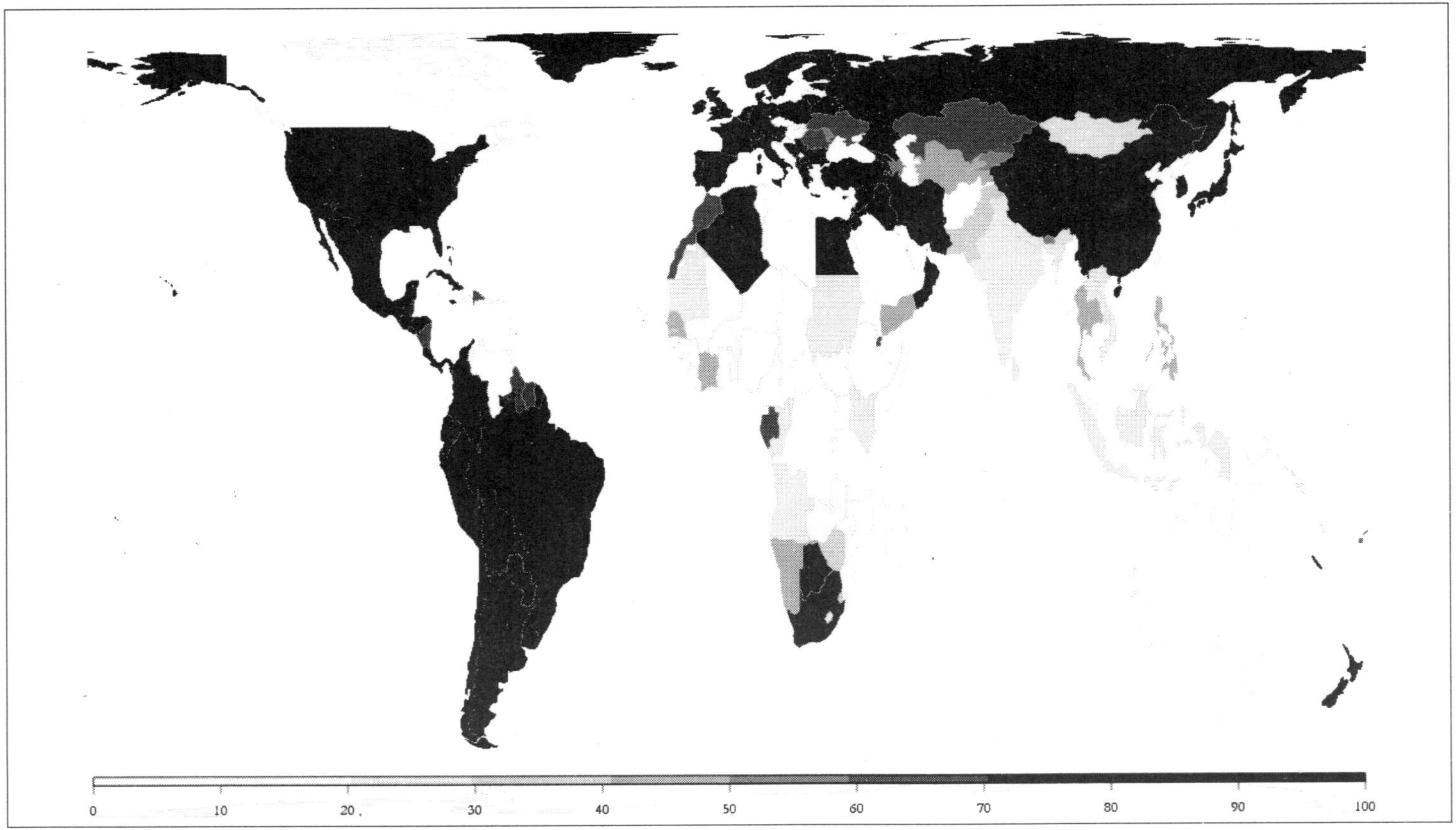

Note: Map plotted using Gall-Peters projection.

WHO/UNICEF Joint Monitoring Programme for Water Supply and Sanitation.

FIGURE 5.2 Proportion of population having access to improved sanitation, 2012 (percent)

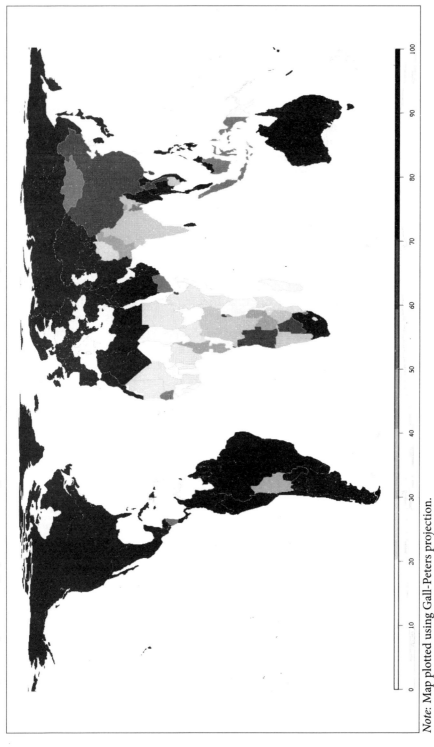

Note: Map plotted using Gall-Peters projection.
Source: Based on data from WHO–UNICEF Joint Monitoring Programme for Water Supply and Sanitation.

Box 5.1 Sanitation and Malnutrition in India

Lack of safe sanitation is a problem of enormous proportions in India. According to the latest statistics from the WHO–UNICEF Joint Monitoring Programme for Water Supply and Sanitation, India alone accounted for 31 percent of the world's population without access to improved sanitation.

According to the 2011 Census of India, only 44 percent of Indian households had improved sanitation facilities. Among rural households, this proportion was a dismal 28 percent. With lack of toilets and water on household premises, open defecation is widely prevalent in India (Table 5.3). The availability of sanitation facilities in public spaces is also very poor. In 2013–14, about 13 percent of India's schools had no toilets (NUEPA, 2014).

Lack of sanitation has important gender and social dimensions. Lack of sanitation facilities at home specifically inconveniences women, exposes them to the worst forms of sexual violence, and harms their health even more than for men (Kulkarni, O'Reilly, and Bhat, 2014; Sharma, Aasaavari, and Anand, 2015). National statistics also show continued disparities in access to sanitation across caste and social groups (Chawla, 2014; Singh, 2014; Swaminathan and Singh, 2014; Thorat, 2009). In a detailed sociological study of determinants of access to basic amenities in rural India, Singh (2014) shows that social exclusion in rural India, particularly as seen in the segregation of residential areas among different social groups, and continued economic differences contribute to continued social and caste disparities in access to sanitation, safe drinking water, and other basic amenities.

Statistical evidence shows that poor access to safe water, sanitation, and hygiene are major determinants of nutritional outcomes in India. Detailed statistical analysis by Spears (2013) showed that "open defecation can account for much or all of excess stunting" among children in India.

There is also a huge gap in the access to safe drinking water. According to data from the 2011 Census of India, only 32 percent of Indian households had access to tap water from a treated source. Lack of a safe water source on household premises is a major factor behind the large proportion of Indian households not being able to use safe sanitation facilities. As shown in Figure 5.4, there is a large overlap in regions that have performed poorly in terms of access to sanitation and water.

The national government in India has introduced specific programmes to tackle the problem of sanitation since the mid-1980s. These programmes have mainly focused on providing financial support for the construction of toilets and activities to raise public awareness. Despite a significant increase in public expenditure (Figure 5.3), these programmes have only had limited success in expanding access to safe sanitation. A recent study shows that a significant proportion of toilets constructed under the Total Sanitation Programme, a flagship programme of the national government in the area of sanitation, have ceased to exist and are not in use (Kumar, 2015). In a review of the Total Sanitation Programme, Hueso and Bell (2013) found that "only one in five latrines reportedly constructed since 2001 were in place in 2011. The rest either had become unusable due to bad construction quality and lack of maintenance, or were not fully built in the first place." Lack of synergy between rural water supply programmes and rural sanitation programmes, inadequate emphasis on awareness-building and hygiene education, and lack of community participation have been identified as the main reasons for the lack of success of public sanitation programmes in India.

TABLE 5.3 India: Proportion of households by different types of sanitation facility, 2011 (percent)

Type of sanitation facility	Rural	Urban	Total
Improved sanitation within premises	28	79	44
Water closet	20	73	36
Other types of improved facility	8	6	8
Unimproved sanitation within premises	3	2	3
Use of public toilets	2	6	3
Open defecation	67	13	50
All households	100	100	100

Source: Census of India, 2011.

FIGURE 5.3 India: Per capita public expenditure on water and sanitation, 1992–93 to 2010–11 (ppp US$)

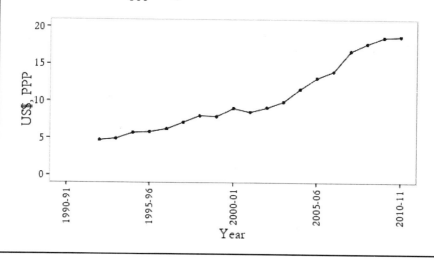

Policy lessons from past experiences

Access to improved sanitation is closely related to the development of public infrastructure for drainage, waste treatment, and waste disposal. In most developing countries, rural sanitation programmes have focused on promoting solutions based on safe on-site sewage disposal because of the impracticality of centralized effluent sewage disposal. Further, the need to

FIGURE 5.4 India: Proportion of houses without access to a water source and toilet on premises, 2011 (percent)

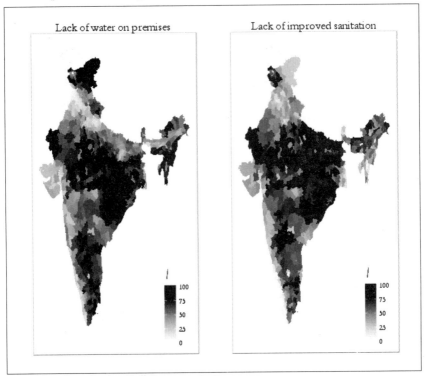

Note: Map plotted using Gall-Peters projection.
Source: Based on data from the Census of India, 2011.

keep costs low has meant the use of low-cost materials that typically are difficult to maintain and clean, thus frustrating the adoption of improved sanitation. Although several technical solutions have been proposed and attempted, the difficulties in maintaining and cleaning low-cost toilets remain an important barrier to widespread adoption of improved sanitation.

In addition, as shown in Figure 5.5, access to improved sanitation is also closely related to supply of piped water to household premises. In general, the existence of piped water supply is a prerequisite for improved household sanitation. Some countries, however, have managed to break this barrier. As shown in Figure 5.5, Sri Lanka, Vietnam, Myanmar, Marshall Islands, Rwanda, and Bangladesh are particularly noteworthy for having achieved significantly above-average levels of access to improved sanitation despite relatively limited access to piped water supply. The figure also shows that, while most high-income countries have good access to piped water on household premises and improved sanitation, several countries have made significant progress in providing access to piped water and improved sanitation despite low per capita income levels.

FIGURE 5.5 Relationship between proportion of population having access to piped water on premises, proportion of population having access to improved sanitation, and per capita income across countries, 2012

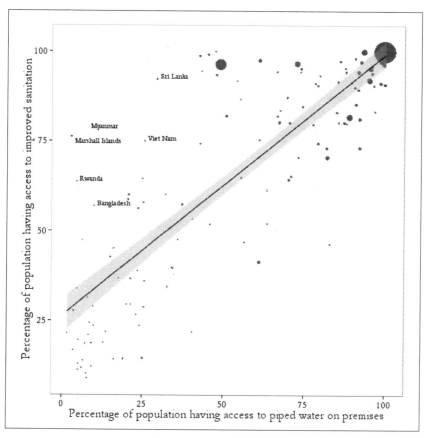

Note: Points for different countries have been sized according to the per capita GDP of the country.

Source: Based on 2012 data from WHO–UNICEF Joint Monitoring Programme for Water Supply and Sanitation.

A large body of empirical literature from across the world has found a significant positive impact of education, in particular women's, on the adoption of improved sanitation. Policymakers, civil society activists and researchers have all highlighted the importance of building awareness for improving sanitation.

In recent years, an alternative approach called Community-led Total Sanitation (CLTS) has been implemented in many countries. Having its origin in a micro-level programme in Bangladesh, CLTS was mainstreamed by the Water and Sanitation Programme (WSP) led by the World Bank, and implemented in twenty-five countries across Asia and Africa. Since the early 1990s, the WSP started to move away from supporting public programmes that provided subsidized toilets to households without toilets. It started supporting CLTS programmes since the early 2000s, and adopted CLTS as the main approach for sanitation programmes by the end of the decade.

CLTS is based on the idea that lack of adoption of improved sanitation in a community is not due to economic deprivation or exclusion from public services, but because of the unwillingness of people to stop defecating in the open. Proponents of CLTS have argued that public support for providing toilets is ineffective and should be *substituted* by community-level interventions to bring about behavioural change, while putting the onus of mobilizing resources for constructing sanitation facilities on the households themselves (Kar and Chambers, 2008; Kar and Pasteur, 2005; Robinson, 2005; Sanan and Moulik, 2007). In a major study on why progress in adoption of improved sanitation in India has been slow, Coffey *et al.* (2014) claimed that people prefer open defecation because they find it "pleasurable".

There are two aspects of the strategy adopted by the CLTS programmes implemented in various countries. First, under these programmes, be-havioural change is brought about by exposing persons practising open defecation to shame, public humiliation, and various kinds of punishment. Monetary fines and humiliating punishments like forcing the offenders to clean public places are imposed on those who engage in open defecation. These are expected to humiliate and coerce people to build toilet facilities, and to stop defecating in the open. Secondly, it is argued that people value and use toilets only if they pay for building them. Toilets built with public subsidies lie unused because people do not value them and see no benefit in using them (Sanan and Moulik, 2007). Thus, no public support is provided for the construction of toilets, existing programmes that provide financial support are to be discontinued, and households are to mobilize their own resources for the construction of toilets. In sum, under CLTS, the focus of intervention is on preventing the practice of open defecation, so that people are left with no choice but to find resources to build toilets for themselves.

Evidence suggests that economic progress does not automatically trans-late into improved sanitation. Experience from sanitation programmes across the world shows that mere provision of funds for the construction of low-cost toilets is not sufficient for the adoption of improved sanitation. However, the fact remains that the vast majority of those who lack improved sanitation are poor, have low levels of educational attainment, and do not have access to public infrastructure for water and drainage on their household premises. Hence, their inability to have or to use a toilet has to be seen as a deprivation and a failure of entitlements rather than as an exercise of freedom.

Recent studies, including from the World Bank, doubt that behavioural changes alone can bring about the requisite increase in the use of improved sanitation. The 2015 *World Development Report* argued that "a program to change social norms about sanitation in these two countries was important but not sufficient to end open defecation" (World Bank, 2015). It took the position that programmes aiming for behavioural change "can complement, but perhaps not substitute for, programmes that provide resources for building toilets" (World Bank, 2015).

Assessing sanitation programmes in Bangladesh, often cited by proponents of CLTS, Black and Fawcett (2008) point out that progress in Bangladesh is not merely because of CLTS, but has much to do with sustained political commitment at the highest level, sustained efforts of the Department of Public Health Engineering and NGOs, and various specific socio-economic and ecological conditions. A comparative assessment of sanitation outcomes in CLTS and non-CLTS villages in Bangladesh by Hanchett *et al.* (2011) showed a substantial increase in the adoption of improved sanitation in all areas, and no significant difference between CLTS and non-CLTS villages. The study concluded that "the government's commitment may have been the cornerstone for influencing the social norms in favor of improved sanitation behaviors and facilities, regardless of the specific approach". Black and Fawcett (2008) strongly argue against using CLTS as a magic bullet to deal with the problem of sanitation regardless of national contexts.

Given that the inability to have or use toilets fundamentally reflects a failure of entitlements, the ethical underpinnings of using humiliation, policing, punishments, and coercion rather than focusing on provision of sanitation facilities along with education, literacy, and sustained awareness-building are questionable. A detailed study of CLTS programmes in Indonesia found that "it is primarily the poor who are the 'targets' of this intervention and that they are, in effect, punished for their poverty and local practices" (Engel and Susilo, 2014). Engel and Susilo (2014) conclude that "CLTS is clearly a very intrusive process involving facilitators from outside the village inspecting individual households and shaming predominantly poor individuals and households for their circumstances and local practices."

Experiences from countries that have made significant advances in access to safe water and improved sanitation suggest that political commitment at the highest level, involvement of all levels of government, sustained fiscal support for the development of common infrastructure and household-level facilities, and a major thrust in awareness-building programmes hold the key to success in the area. Community participation in raising awareness and building a social commitment to sanitation has always been crucial. It is important to design solutions keeping in mind the local context, including both constraints and resources, rather than imposing one-size-fits-all technical or economic solutions. Improvement in the area of sanitation often goes hand in hand with improvement in access to water on the household premises. This is particularly important for rural areas, where the gap in access to water supply on household premises is substantial in many countries. In such countries, programmes for development of domestic water supply and sanitation in rural areas should be planned and implemented together.

Box 5.2 ICN2 Framework for Action: Recommended actions on water, sanitation and hygiene

- Recommendation 50: Implement policies and programmes using participatory approaches to improve water management in agriculture and food production.[a]

- Recommendation 51: Invest in and commit to achieve universal access to safe drinking water, with the participation of civil society and the support of international partners, as appropriate.

- Recommendation 52: Implement policies and strategies using participatory approaches to ensure universal access to adequate sanitation[b] and to promote safe hygiene practices, including hand washing with soap.

---

[a] Including by reducing water wastage in irrigation, strategies for multiple use of water (including waste water), and better use of appropriate technology.
[b] Including by implementing effective risk assessment and management practices on safe waste water use and sanitation.

6

Governance: Accelerating and Sustaining Momentum

Much has changed in recent years, bringing nutrition to the forefront of the global development agenda. In 2008, the worst food-price spike in a generation compelled political leaders across the globe to rethink assumptions and received wisdom about the capacity of economic growth alone to address food access and malnutrition problems. A series of articles published at the same time in *The Lancet* provided new evidence demonstrating the high human and economic costs of malnutrition, and issued a clarion call for reform of what the authors of a paper on international action against undernutrition described as the "fragmented and dysfunctional" "international nutrition system" (Morris, Cogill, and Uauy, 2008).

Soon afterward, in 2010, the Scaling Up Nutrition (SUN) movement was born, a new type of multi-stakeholder and multisectoral partnership initiative launched under the administrative aegis of the UN Secretary-General (United Nations, 2012), but with a decidedly open and flexible governance structure that allows it to be called a movement rather than a UN initiative or programme. In a relatively short period of time, SUN has also garnered the active involvement of major donors and more than 100 major organizations organized into four networks: donors, civil society, the private sector, and UN system agencies, funds, and programmes. The SUN movement seeks to organize itself around the priorities of countries that have subscribed as members of the movement. By June 2015, SUN had attracted 55 countries to its ranks.[1]

---

[1] The SUN website states: "SUN is a country-led Movement, which puts countries at the heart of global efforts to improve nutrition." Available at: www.scalingupnutrition.org/sun-countries.

Owing in part to the well-organized advocacy of SUN and bolstered by a second series of *Lancet* articles published in 2013, a variety of complementary initiatives have been launched, including the June 2013 Nutrition for Growth Summit, which focused attention on nutrition and mobilized more than US$4.15 billion in public investment commitments, along with US$19 billion in nutrition-sensitive investments, between 2013 and 2020;[2] the launch of the Global Panel on Agriculture and Food Systems for Nutrition at the same time; and the commitment to publish the *Global Nutrition Report*, first published in November 2014 and produced under the editorial aegis of the International Food Policy Research Institute (IFPRI) with contributions from across the global nutrition community.

In July 2014, the UN General Assembly's Open Working Group on Sustainable Development Goals produced a report calling for 17 new Sustainable Development Goals (SDGs) and 169 targets. That report has been subsequently accepted as the basis, with only minor technical adjustments, for the post-2015 development agenda that will be adopted by the UN member-states at a special summit in September 2015. The new SDGs include at least six headline goals and eighteen targets materially relevant to nutrition, including not only targets that specifically mention nutrition, but also targets such as poverty eradication, improved food systems, women's empowerment, and improved access to safe water and sanitation – which, when combined, present a comprehensive approach not only to enhance efforts on nutrition, but also to address its underlying causes. While the process may only endorse one or two indicators of malnutrition, the potential number of nutrition-related indicators may be much larger.

In light of these developments, the Second International Conference on Nutrition (ICN2), which took place in Rome in November 2014, represented a culminating event. Jointly organized by the Food and Agriculture Organization and the World Health Organization, both United Nations specialized agencies, ICN2 was an effort to integrate and unify a broad range of activities within a defined set of intergovernmentally endorsed political commitments, and to provide a flexible and comprehensive framework for action. Achieving broad agreement among the world's nation-states is always a challenge, and is made even more challenging when the issues are as complex as they are with nutrition. Thus, while ICN2's two outcomes – the Rome Declaration and Framework for Action – did not break new ground in knowledge or policy, they made a major contribution to nutrition action by forging a new intergovernmental consensus on the needed scale and scope for adequate policy action.

---

[2] "Nutrition for Growth Commitments: Executive Summary". Available at www.gov.uk/government/uploads/system/uploads/attachment_data/file/207274/nutrition-for-growth-commitments.pdf.

The ICN2 has thus given impetus to efforts to reform and adapt existing institutional arrangements for coordination of collective action at global, regional, and national levels. It has been a timely reassertion of the universal relevance of nutrition issues, and has established an inclusive balance among the broad array of policy and technical emphases extant in the revival of nutrition activity across the globe. The ICN2, in short, was a summing up and ratification by the largest meeting of governments and non-state actors assembled against malnutrition in history. It marks the climax of the agenda-setting phase of nutrition activism and heralds the next phase: a concerted collective action to improve nutrition across the world.

Déjà vu?

Does this mean that all the 'heavy lifting' has been completed to build political momentum for a major breakthrough on nutrition? From past experience the answer is no. This is not the first time that the world community, armed with new evidence of the developmental consequences of malnutrition and new policy approaches, has attempted to put nutrition at the forefront of the global development agenda. A real breakthrough is possible but, to realize this potential, further action is necessary to overcome the forces of political inertia that have doomed past global initiatives on malnutrition.

At least twice before, about two decades apart, the world community has rallied around a new or renewed vision of the relevance of nutrition for development. In the early 1970s, the then World Bank President Robert McNamara called for a reorientation in the Bank's mission, shifting emphasis to poverty reduction. In his annual address to the Bank's Board of Governors on 27 September 1971, McNamara described malnutrition as "a major barrier to human development" and said to the finance ministers of the world: "the central conclusion I wish to propose to you is that the international development community and the individual governments of the countries concerned must face up to the importance and implications of the nutrition problem" (cited in Herforth and Hoberg, 2014, p. 8). The new emphasis on improved nutrition as essential for development was supported by the scientific finding of the previous decade that malnutrition could lead to lifelong physical and cognitive impairment, and was given additional political impetus by the world food crisis created by the food price spike of 1972–73.

In the event, however, World Bank executives and development specialists were uneasy about the idea of investing in nutrition, and embedded the new nutrition emphasis in work on integrated rural development. The result was a flourishing programmatic emphasis on multisectoral planning in which nutrition targets and monitoring were seldom well-defined (Herforth and Hoberg, 2014, p. 11). By the end of the 1970s and in the early 1980s, both integrated rural development and its handmaiden, multisectoral planning for nutrition, were in crisis for having failed to produce significant results. Both would soon be abandoned altogether in the face of the developing country debt and financial crises that led to the end of nearly all major forms of development planning and policy interventions; deep cuts in government budgets, staffs, and services; and a growing belief among donors and governments that all economic and social problems, including nutrition, would be solved by market-induced growth.

By the early 1990s, the high food and commodity prices of the early 1970s were long gone, and an era of abundant, low-cost world food supply was expected to lead to progressive alleviation of malnutrition and food insecurity. When this did not happen, efforts were once again renewed to draw world attention to the key developmental importance of addressing malnutrition, including both undernutrition and undernourishment. The 1992 International Conference on Nutrition (ICN) drew attention to the former, and the 1996 World Food Summit (WFS) to the latter.

Despite the absence of a trigger event such as the 1972–73, or the 2008, 2010–11, and 2012 food-price spikes, these two global conferences of the 1990s did contribute to a broader awareness that the problems of undernutrition and undernourishment could not be solved by the availability of food alone. Special interventions, it was recognized, would be needed to address the economic, social, and environmental causes of malnutrition, and to ensure access to safe food.[3] The ICN also helped to spur renewed commitment to nutrition as a key public objective. The 1992 World Declaration on Nutrition included a pledge to "eliminate hunger and reduce all forms of malnutrition", and the accompanying Plan of Action for Nutrition called for a revival or strengthening of planning through a new generation of National Plans of Action for Nutrition (NPANs). The ICN delegates committed "to revise or prepare, before the end of 1994, our national plans of action, including attainable goals and measurable targets, based on the principles and the relevant strategies in the Plan of Action" (Nishida, 2013). Based on analyses of country situations, the NPANs reintroduced multisectoral thinking, and were to be developed with broad participation from governments, both national and local, NGOs, and the private sector. The initial results were promising. A 1995 FAO survey found that by 1994, 54 countries had completed NPANs, and that progress was being made in another 71 countries.[4]

---

[3] The concept of "hidden hunger" to describe micronutrient deficiencies gained currency through the 1991 Montreal conference on 'Ending Hidden Hunger', jointly organized by the WHO, UNICEF, and the World Bank.
[4] The experience with NPANs is usefully summarized, with reference to several sources, in Mokoro (2015), Annex I: Issues and Lessons in Multi-Sector Planning.

FIGURE 6.1 The political economy of malnutrition

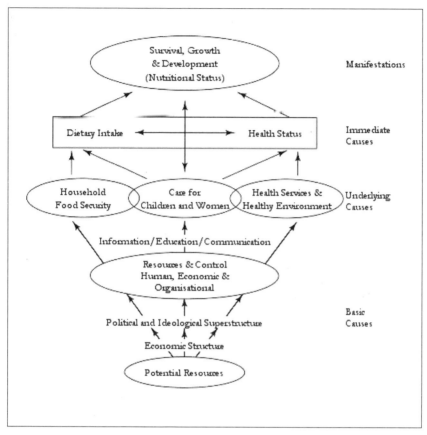

Source: UNICEF (1990).

The 1990s' effort took place in an era when planning and state interventions, more generally, were discouraged. Still, nutrition experts recognized and continued to emphasize that malnutrition has many causes, and that addressing it requires concerted actions to improve systems for production, including processing, of food, health, sanitation, and water. Figure 6.1 reproduces an iconic diagram of the linkages between basic, underlying, and immediate causes of malnutrition that was first presented in a Policy Review submitted to the UNICEF Executive Board in March 1990, and that remains, in various iterations, a touchstone of nutrition policy discussion today.[5] Here, in the language of the time, the multiple causes of malnutrition are elegantly mapped with different horizontal layers that begin with deep, "basic" causes that include economic and social exclusion, discrimination

---

[5] UNICEF. E/ICEF/1990/L.6, 9 March 1990. Diagram reprinted from Mokoro (2015), Annex I, p. 282.

or vulnerability. These link to unequal control over resources and result in "underlying" causes – impacts on households, and health and sanitation systems – that in turn contribute to "immediate" causes of malnutrition in the form of mutually reinforcing factors of inadequate dietary intake and disease. All these causes culminate ultimately in malnutrition and premature death.

Yet there were few takers outside of the "nutrition community" for a comprehensive approach, and the period has become known retrospectively as the era of "nutrition isolation" – a time when the nutrition community found itself forced to go it alone. Nutrition work became more narrowly focused on addressing micronutrient deficiencies through nutrition-specific interventions, where, it was believed, linkages between actions and results could be more effectively demonstrated. In the end, the second cycle of global nutrition efforts ended with an echo of the first. Few NPANs were ever implemented, international coordination became increasingly fractured and competitive, interventions became more micro- and project-oriented, and donor support ever harder to find.

Seen in perspective, the current moment appears less unique, less "unprecedented", with the risk of failure more real and more worrisome. There is, to be sure, much in the present context that can be used to make a case that this time is different. The strength of the underlying science and accumulation of country- and context-specific evidence; the breadth and level of donor support; the availability of a new set of policy instruments classed as "social protection" to address some of the basic and underlying causes of malnutrition; the entry of a host of new social actors in the form of NGOs, CSOs, well-endowed philanthropies, and new social movements; and the emergence of new partnership initiatives such as the SUN movement: all herald a potential for effective action that is arguably far greater than at any time in the past. But the question is whether these factors alone can overcome the political impediments and inertia that overwhelmed past efforts to achieve an accelerated impact to reduce malnutrition. These impediments and inertia have less to do with the availability of knowledge and evidence, or benevolent intentions, and much more to do with nutrition governance – or, to put it another way, the political economy of nutrition action.

Confronting the political economy of nutrition

Today, the main sources of friction and inertia remain the same ones that have repeatedly undermined nutrition efforts in the past. Nutrition advocates agree on at least five large and persistent causes of nutrition failure over the years. First, those who suffer most from malnutrition, almost by definition, are the marginal and disadvantaged; in nearly all countries, they are an uninfluential minority, even where malnutrition is widespread, and where those who suffer from malnutrition normally lack a voice and the capacity for effective political action. Thus, national political incentives to address malnutrition are inherently and persistently weak. In the battle for high-level policy attention, the forces of political inertia work constantly to suppress nutrition in "a low-priority cycle" (Natalicchio *et al.*, 2009).

Secondly, effective solutions require actions by a wide variety of actors from different ministries, agencies, and organizations, including private sector entities and other non-state actors, with different disciplines and different narratives for both causes and solutions, and with different and often competing institutional priorities and interests.[6] Bringing and holding "the nutrition community" together, accordingly, will be no mean feat. Fragmentation and rivalry are in-built and cannot be wished away. Seasoned hands and conventional wisdom both caution against policy and program-matic initiatives that depend on high levels of cross-sectoral coordination and collaboration: the organizational barriers to such collaboration are both "durable and strong" and "the risk is too great that such coordination will not happen".[7]

Thirdly, the risks and challenges of engaging the private sector, especially the large transnational food and drink corporations that dominate global processed-food production and distribution, present a special set of major challenges for an inclusive, 'big tent' approach to mobilizing nutrition action. The record of hostility to the public regulation of producers of unhealthy processed food and drinks, and their ongoing efforts to circumvent established norms and regulations in both developed and developing countries – e.g., the International Code of Marketing of Breast-milk Substitutes – make issues of conflict of interest a source of deep concern and division.[8] These concerns are not without warrant. A literature review

---

[6] James Levinson once identified at least five different groups in "the nutrition community", each with its own interests and narratives. Levinson's list was far from exhaustive, and failed to include public health nutritionists and agriculturalists. See "Institutionalization of Nutrition: International Nutrition in Search of an Institutional Home", in Gillespie, McLachlan, and Shrimpton (2003). See also Reich and Balarajan (2012).

[7] Benson (2011), cited in Reich and Balarajan (2012).

[8] To address these concerns, and additional concerns that the SUN movement's own approach to conflict of interest is much too permissive, the Geneva-based Global Social Observatory (GSO) was requested to conduct a Consultation Process on Conflict of Interest in the SUN movement. The Final Report of the consultation, published in April 2015, included the following observation: "There is a fundamental inconsistency between the SUN Principles of Engagement and the varied national approaches to implementing the International Code of Marketing of Breast-milk Substitutes. Consistent, authoritative guidance is neededistent, authoritative guidance is needed from 'those with the mandates at the global level'." The work of GSO itself raises questions about the attempt to regulate action through promulgation of principles. In a comment in the *British Medical Journal*, Judith Richter notes that the approach taken by GSO blurs key distinctions between diverging opinions among actors, differing fiduciary responsibilities

in *The Lancet* found no evidence that self-regulation by industry or public–private partnerships enhances policy effectiveness or food quality and safety, but provided significant evidence of the ways that engagement with the private sector served to distort or undermine public health policies and programmes (Moodie *et al.*, 2013). The authors identified several strategies used by large companies to deflect public attention from the negative health effects of highly processed foods, and to block or divert efforts at regulation: distortion and bias of research;[9] cooptation of policymakers and health professionals; intense lobbying against public regulation including direct attacks on WHO and other international organizations; and public or social marketing campaigns designed to shape public opinion, for example, by reframing public health issues as issues of consumer or personal choice. The authors of the review concluded that any engagement with the private sector must include strong firewalls against private sector engagement in policy and regulatory issues – a recommendation that has been fiercely resisted both by industry and by many donor governments. Advocacy for a broad partnership approach that includes a strong appeal to private sector inclusion must deal with these concerns, and demonstrate that any mechanisms established to foster private sector engagement in nutrition action will be backed by firewalls and active monitoring to avoid undermining key public policy objectives.

Fourthly, despite the critical importance of nutrition for development and mounting evidence of the high value-for-money of nutrition investments, nutrition has no natural institutional home and, therefore, no natural champion. Delivery of nutrition services is normally the responsibility of agencies or ministries such as agriculture, health, sanitation, social services, or water, which, in many cases, do not see nutrition as a primary responsibility or a primary interest of their constituencies.

The fifth factor is the matter of capacity, not just for the design of high-quality, potentially high-impact nutrition policy, but especially for the more challenging and costly implementation and management of those policies, as well as the patient building of institutions through which policies are supported. Achieving the required global expansion of nutrition actions depends on many things going well, and on many people acquiring the requisite knowledge, skills, and resources. Building capacity is a slow process that can be accelerated only with substantial international cooperation. Too often, especially in countries with a heavy burden of malnutrition, sustained

---

of market-led and public-interest actors, and conflicts of interest pertaining to individual or institutional vested interests. "This blurred terminology," she adds, "hinders SUN participants' understanding of the ultimate aim of conflict of interest policies: i.e., the protection of integrity, independence and public trust in persons and institutions serving public interests" (Richter, 2015).

[9] See also Rowe *et al.* (2009).

nutrition action depends on sustained financing, which is only possible through sustained external support.

All five factors work continuously, like gravity, to weigh down nutrition action. To overcome them, strong levers are needed that go beyond focus and commitment. In the remainder of this chapter, we address three groups of questions concerning the political economy of nutrition governance, and particularly focus on the role of the multilateral system as a promoter, sustainer, and enabler of country-level commitment and action to provide answers to them.

Key issues in global governance for nutrition

A first set of questions asks: how can the political momentum gained in recent years be sustained against the persistently powerful economic, social, and environmental forces that work to disperse and undo nutrition efforts over time? Achieving nutrition impacts is a work of years, if not decades, with measures that must be monitored over half-decades and longer. Policy must be sustained beyond a single champion in the presidency or a leading ministry, and must survive regular changes in government. Against the prevailing forces of entropy, the case for focused, sustained action and investment in nutrition must be made repeatedly, and government and donor propensities to change emphases must be resisted or overcome. The need for complementary action across sectors does not by itself automatically give rise to coordinated planning; rather it presents a recurring challenge to governments and their constituencies.

Secondly, if a global strategy and effort are required, how can the world community best organize to sustain a significant effort over at least a decade and beyond? In particular, what can and must be done at the global and regional levels to enable effective action at the country level? What institutional arrangements and structures are required to support this activity? And how can these activities and structures adapt or respond to new information and events?

Thirdly, what are the appropriate roles and expected contributions of United Nations agencies, funds and programmes, and allied international organizations, in a world of many more and diverse development partners whose collective resources dwarf those that can be mobilized by the UN system alone? Should the UN agencies be counted as simply one among many partners for countries, or should there be a differentiation of roles based on the unique responsibilities and accountability of UN agencies in relation to member-states? One important potential role of the UN agencies, which follows from their unique standing in the multilateral system, is to serve as facilitator and coordinator of international support. But is it realistic for agencies that also seek donor funds to serve as neutral and trusted facilitators of actions? Do the agencies themselves want to play this role, especially if playing it would restrict their own fund-raising activities? Since they cannot establish a credible field presence without strong donor support, it would be self-defeating for UN entities to focus exclusively on normative and policy guidance, and eschew any responsibility for delivery or implementation.

Overcoming inertia: The vital contribution of Sustainable Development Goals

In developing answers to these questions, we focus particularly on the role of global governance – the multilateral, especially UN-centred, processes and institutions that help to set norms, standards, and expectations, provide appropriate (non-prescriptive, norm-based) policy guidance, enable measurement and monitoring of standardized results, mobilize resources and facilitate coordinated action by many actors across sectors and disciplines.

Ultimately, most effective actions to improve nutrition outcomes take place at the country level rather than at the regional or global level. But it is a fallacy to assert that global and regional advocacy and coordination efforts are therefore necessarily redundant, inefficient or ineffective, and therefore a dispensable means of sustaining effective country-level action. To overcome the forces of inertia and fragmentation, it is vital to recognize that important action needs to be taken at all levels, including the international and regional levels, to sustain high-level national political attention to nutrition. Attending only to the national level may weaken nutrition champions and leave them without important sources of information, guidance, and moral and financial support when they confront strong national inertia, political competition and complexity, and powerful institutional rivalries. The potential for effective national action, as the experience of the UN Millennium Development Goals (MDGs) shows, can be greatly strengthened and sustained by an international milieu that provides strong norms; simplified, consistent, flexible, and adaptable policy guidance; facilities for knowledge and experience-sharing among political leaders; resources for building technical and institutional capacity; and comparable data for measuring and monitoring progress.

One of the most important vehicles for building a global milieu for sustained nutrition action, therefore, is the post-2015 development agenda, at whose core are the 17 Sustainable Development Goals (SDGs) and their 169 Targets. Nutrition looms large in the new framework. As noted earlier, the SDGs, which will formally be adopted by the UN member-states in September 2015, contain at least six goals and eighteen targets that are materially related to nutrition outcomes. Together, they work at all levels of the political economy of nutrition outlined in Figure 6.1, addressing 'basic' issues of social and economic marginalization such as women's empowerment and access to resources; "underlying" causes, such as weak systems for food and water access, health, and sanitation; and immediate causes, such as inadequate uptake and absorption of nutrients, and diseases that are both the cause and consequence of malnutrition. The question, of course, is how can action on all these fronts be best organized and sustained?

For many observers, the sheer number of goals and targets in the new SDGs has itself become a major cause of bewilderment and criticism. In a published comment in *The Lancet*, the editor Richard Horton gave pointed expression to these concerns: "The SDGs are fairy tales", he wrote, "dressed in the bureaucratese of intergovernmental narcissism, adorned with the robes of multilateral paralysis, and poisoned by the acid of nation-state failure. Yet this is served up as our future" (Horton, 2014). Given the stakes, one can easily understand the frustration, and perhaps even the bitterness, behind such remarks. But these are fundamentally misplaced, reflecting a deep misunderstanding of both the logic and intention behind the successor generation of global development goals.

The new SDGs depart from the previous generation's development agenda in three essential respects. First, they are the product of an intergovernmental process based on the multilateral principle; in other words, they have been written, and owned, by the UN member-states. Secondly, they are intended to be universally relevant and are defined to constitute a global social, economic, and environmental compact that aims to induce ambitious and transformative action, albeit without being prescriptive. They are a vision that reflects language agreed on by consensus of 193 nations, with balances of interests and compromises that reflect contemporary political reality in all its unavoidable complexity. Thirdly, they deliberately eschew the specificity that characterized the previous developmental goals, precisely because it was widely recognized that the segregated, siloed or vertical approaches of the MDGs missed out on key developmental linkages necessary for accelerated impact and long-term sustainability.

The last point bears particular emphasis. There are no true stand-alone goals in the new SDGs, despite the habit of many commentators of describing the headline goals in these terms. On close inspection, each goal is itself an amalgam of several desiderata. SDG 2, for example, reads: "End hunger, achieve food security and improved nutrition, and promote sustainable agriculture." The targets carry the same integrative agenda to another level. Target 2.2 of SDG 2 states: "by 2030 end all forms of malnutrition, including achieving by 2025 the internationally agreed targets on stunting and wasting in children under 5 years of age, and address the nutritional needs of adolescent girls, pregnant and lactating women, and older persons." The goals and targets do in fact set up an extraordinarily ambitious agenda, but provide only limited substantive guidance on how it is to be implemented. For that, a supplement is needed – a trigger to unlock the potential of the new framework, backed by a system that can provide the impetus to action, legitimated norms, time-bound frameworks, appropriate technical and policy guidance, robust monitoring, and mechanisms for systemic learning and adaptation.

Needed: A trigger for unified global support

The key to overcome political fragmentation and inertia, and to sustain action at the national level, paradoxically, lies at the global level. The new SDGs, properly understood, provide a comprehensive and potentially powerful global set of intergovernmentally agreed goals and targets for sustained action over a period of fifteen years – an agenda that comprehensively addresses all the causes of malnutrition. If we look beyond the segregated silos that defined the MDGs, understand that the SDGs are designed to enable the development of broad laterally integrative strategies, and accept that there are therefore no true "stand-alone" goals in the new framework for any sector or "vertical", we could begin to recognize their true value in creating the possibility for sustained action on nutrition.

But to make all these elements cohere, it is essential to consolidate the broad array of political commitments that have been made into a unified framework for action and then back it with an effective set of mechanisms for animating the global commitment to nutrition in all its dimensions. The first task was accomplished with the twin outcomes of ICN2: the Rome Declaration on Nutrition and the Framework for Action. What remains is to provide the trigger, adjust the international architecture for nutrition and energize it.

The natural trigger for following up ICN2 would be the one recommended to the United Nations General Assembly in the Rome Declaration: a ten-year programme of action, which could be branded as a comprehensive UN Decade of Action on Nutrition, supported by all UN institutions, member-states, and allied organizations. A more modest alternative would be to fashion a schedule of UN system reporting under the standard rubric of "follow-up to a major UN conference", that could be designed to tie together the disparate indicators and monitoring of actions and institutional developments for nutrition in the SDGs. The costs of both options would be modest, with most expenses being borne by the respective UN entities out of their own resources in fulfilment of their mandates. The chief difference is at the level of UN system coordination, which depends principally on agencies, funds, and programmes' willingness to work together in support of a global agenda, and also at the level of publicity that can be generated by the UN's

Department of Public Information, which has the capacity to significantly increase the visibility of UN messages at the global scale.

The proposed UN decade met with resistance from countries concerned about making action-commitments on specific topics while the new SDGs were still being negotiated. The second idea would be a fall-back and would likely not receive the high-level publicity that a UN decade typically generates, but could still provide powerful incentives to coordinated action in a UN system called upon to demonstrate that it is "fit for purpose" in supporting the new SDGs. The UN General Assembly adopted a resolution welcoming the ICN2 outcomes on 6 July 2015, but decided at the same time to postpone consideration of follow-up actions, including the question of the decade, until after the conclusion of the SDG Summit in September 2015. By then, it should be clear that supporting the SDGs necessarily implies supporting a broad and ambitious global agenda on all forms of malnutrition – undernourishment, undernutrition, especially micronutrient deficiencies and overweight/obesity.

Whichever course is chosen, the key question will remain: is the UN system[10] really capable of delivering on the promise of the SDGs? Certainly the UN agencies, funds, and programmes cannot undertake to provide all the services needed. Then what is to be their role in enabling and facilitating action by the various other actors comprising "the international nutrition system" today? Why would others accept that role? And how will the UN system organize itself to play this role? There are serious doubts about the UN's approach, as we have noted, and a history of inter-agency rivalry and competition that is still to be overcome. How, then, will the rules of the game be defined and adjusted? How will all nutrition action be monitored so that progress is measured, lessons learned, and success emulated? And how will all parties – including UN system agencies – be recognized for their contributions or their failures?

What is to be done? By whom? And how?

The key requirements for effective action on nutrition are widely recognized. They include sustained political commitment and mobilization of effective nutrition action across sectors; provision of authoritative, evidence-based norms and standards; clear, simple guidance on policy and regulation;

---

[10] The term "United Nations" is inherently ambiguous, as it can refer to either the UN member-states who collectively comprise the United Nations, or to the Secretariat, or both. Thus it is conventional among specialists and diplomats to refer to the "UN system" when referring to the UN specialized agencies, funds, and programmes. This practice is followed herein. The terms "UN system" and "UN agencies" always refer to the specialized agencies of the United Nations including the World Bank and the International Monetary Fund, UN funds, and UN programmes, each of which has its own respective mandates and governing bodies, as well as the United Nations Secretariat, led by the Secretary-General.

selection and monitoring of appropriate indicators of progress toward desired nutrition outcomes; progressive development of institutional as well as individual capacities, including for strategic leadership and innovation; and, of course, sustained mobilization of resources to support large-scale change.

Of these, there are a number of tasks that can be performed most efficiently or most effectively at the global or supra-national levels: agreement on appropriate shared norms, goals, and targets; formulating clear, implementable policy and guidance; setting nutrition, food, and safety standards; systematic learning from diverse experiences; selection of indicators and design of instruments for tracking progress against key targets; and monitoring and reporting on national, regional, and global performance. This is the stuff of global governance. Each of these services has a public goods aspect in that it is unlikely to be supplied privately, and needs an internationally legitimated process or institution to support it. But this is not the same as providing all these goods by public institutions alone.

A vital development in contemporary international governance has been the increasingly widespread practice of linking intergovernmental institutions and processes to multistakeholder platforms that make the process of developing and providing these services more open and inclusive, a shared responsibility of diverse social actors. The same development also makes international rule-making more complex and demanding. And all this in an era when funding for such public purposes has long been scarce. Thus, the question of what needs to be done quickly gives way to the questions, who is going to do all this and how? Specifically, which international institutions are going to be responsible for which activities? Which are shared responsibilities and which not? How are such activities to be coordinated and by whom? Who is to be held accountable and by whom?

Towards a new international architecture for nutrition

To establish a viable framework for the kind of broad and ambitious global agenda on nutrition suggested by ICN2 outcomes, it is useful, first, to think in terms of key functions, and then ask how existing institutions already fulfil, or can be adapted, streamlined or strengthened to perform these functions in the most efficient manner possible. Box 6.1 summarizes the main functions to be performed in a working global institutional framework that is adequate to the range of tasks to be performed. It then identifies existing institutions that can support these functions, the main responsibilities that each institution currently has or could take on, and also the mechanisms that exist for making each of these institutions accountable to the member-states. Nearly all of these accountability mechanisms are intergovernmental in nature, and most embody the UN's multilateral principle of sovereign equality, meaning that the rules are made and oversight conducted in a system in which all states have an equal voice and vote. A key aspect of the proposed architecture, in other words, is that nearly all of its elements are linked to a multilateral intergovernmental process that governs its design and operations, and assesses its impact.

This institutional architecture, for the most part, already exists. At the apex of the system stands the UN General Assembly (UNGA), the world's most inclusive and authoritative intergovernmental deliberative forum. UNGA decisions, carried by consensus, reflect the general will of the global community and therefore considerable political legitimacy, even if, like in all legislative bodies, they bear the imprint of conflict and compromise. The UNGA, directly or through delegated authorities, sets the global development agenda on terms mutually agreed by developed and developing countries, and thereby determines the priorities of UN agencies, funds, and programmes. The prolonged process to define a new post-2015 development agenda, with SDGs at the core, is fundamental for global governance, embracing not only prioritized goals and targets, but also institutional frameworks for implementation, monitoring, and evaluation. Major intergovernmental conferences, such as the 2012 Conference on Sustainable Development, are often mandated by the UNGA, and the outcomes of such conferences are not considered fully endorsed by the UN member-states unless they are explicitly confirmed by a subsequent UNGA resolution. The ICN2 outcomes were formally welcomed by the UNGA on 6 July 2015.[11]

While deliberating on the new development agenda, UN member-states devoted considerable attention to implementation issues, and recognized the need for a robust system for monitoring, reporting, and evaluating progress. A major institutional innovation for monitoring SDGs during the next fifteen years is the establishment of the High Level Political Forum (HLPF), an annual review process in which government ministers or, quadrennially, heads of state and government meet to review evidence, share experiences, and deliberate on appropriate policy responses. The principal objective of the HLPF is to ensure ongoing and high-level member-state attention to the effectiveness of policies implemented, and other actions taken to improve progress towards the established goals and targets.[12] Ministerial meetings will take place under the auspices of the UN Economic and Social Council, a principal intergovernmental organ of the United Nations; quadrennial meetings with heads of states and governments will take place in the General Assembly. UN agencies, funds, and programmes provide the needed data and reporting, and support the UN Secretariat in accordance with their respective mandates.

---

[11] UNGA resolution A/RES/69/310, available at www.un.org/en/ga/69/resolutions.shtml.
[12] UNGA Resolution A/RES/66/288, "The Future We Want", paragraphs 84–86.

Box 6.1 Functions, Institutions, Responsibilities, and Accountability for Nutrition Governance

---

Set global goals, targets and indicators

- *Process/Institution*: SDGs/UN General Assembly

- *Key responsibilities*:

    - Define global schedule of developmental priorities with integrated economic, social and environmental objectives

    - Ensure broad stakeholder consultation

    - Establish indicators and framework for ongoing global monitoring and reporting

    - Promote and track international cooperation toward shared ends

- *Accountability*

    - Mutual accountability among sovereign member-states within framework of voluntary commitments, mutual reporting

Make national political commitments and develop comprehensive framework for action on nutrition

- *Process/Institution*: ICN2 (Member-States Conference), jointly organized by WHO and FAO and endorsed by UN General Assembly resolution

- *Key responsibilities*:

    - Provide definitive member-states' commitments

    - Provide comprehensive framework for action as policy guidance

    - Enable participation of civil society and private sector in preparatory and follow-up processes

- *Accountability*

    - Mutual accountability of member-states and partners through follow-up process to be determined by UN General Assembly

Provide ongoing oversight of and mutual sharing/learning from national experiences

- *Process/Institution*: High Level Political Forum – UN General Assembly for quadrennial meetings of heads of state or government; Economic and Social Council (EcoSoc) for other annual meetings

- *Key responsibilities*:

    - Monitor performance/outcomes on SDGs

    - Facilitate experience sharing and learning on a voluntary basis

    - Identify emerging issues and propose new actions

- *Accountability*

  - Voluntary national reporting and review through UN Regional Commissions and voluntary reporting; high-level policy review and experience sharing; changing topical focus

Provide specialized norms and policy guidance for food security and nutrition; science-policy interface; specialized global monitoring and analysis for food security and nutrition

- *Process/Institution*: Committee on World Food Security and Nutrition (CFS) supported by multistakeholder Advisory Group, High Level Panel of Experts (HLPE) and joint secretariat of FAO, IFAD, and WFP

- *Key responsibilities*:

  - Stand-alone specialized forum for review and analysis of global outcomes

  - Multistakeholder forum, including civil society and private sector, for generation of norms and policy guidance on food security and nutrition

  - Specialized entity (HLPE) for review of nutrition science on agreed topics

- *Accountability*

  - Ultimate decision-making authority rests with member-states, who are accountable for decisions and outcomes; reports main findings and activities to EcoSoc

Develop global programme of action to support integration of nutrition-related SDGs and targets, within ICN2 commitments and framework for action

- *Process/Institution*: Decade or multi-year programme of action on nutrition declared by UN General Assembly, with inter-agency coordination by FAO and WHO, supported by UN SCN Members and Secretariat

- *Key responsibilities*:

  - Documentation and review of global commitments on nutrition

  - Gap analysis, identification of opportunities for streamlining and improving impact

  - Publication of synoptic programme of action taking into account commitments at national, regional and global levels

  - Tracking of programmatic initiatives at country, regional and global levels

  - Preparation of regular periodic reports on actions taken and outcomes

  - Raising awareness for global norms and standards

- *Accountability*

  – Reporting to and review by UNGA, EcoSoc or HLPF as directed in resolution on a UN decade or ten-year programme of action; FAO and WHO would be lead coordinating UN agencies, owing to their joint role in organizing ICN2

Coordination of UN system activities in support of global action for nutrition

- *Process/Institution*: (Reformed) UN Standing Committee on Nutrition: UN and allied international organizations with substantial mandates in nutrition and nutrition-sensitive areas

- *Key responsibilities*:

  – Streamlined to focus on inter-agency coordination of inputs to global nutrition and related processes

  – Monitoring and coordination of UN-system global activities in support of SDGs and ICN2 follow-up, including ten-year programme of action

  – Guidance to UN system agencies and allied institutions for implementation of global norms and standards in UN-supported operations; monitoring of adherence

  – Internet presence: single point of entry to UN system resources, tools and instruments for nutrition support

- *Accountability*

  – UNSCN activity would be reported to EcoSoc; could be reviewed by CFS and reported through CFS to EcoSoc

  – UN SCN member organizations are accountable to their respective governing bodies (e.g., World Health Assembly for WHO)

Coordination of UN system advocacy on nutrition and related subjects under aegis of the UN Secretary-General's Zero Hunger Challenge (ZHC)

- *Process/Institution*: UN Secretary-General's High Level Task Force on Global Food Security and Nutrition (HLTF) – 22 UN agencies, funds, and programmes, OECD, and WTO

- *Key responsibilities*:

  – Coordinate HLTF members' advocacy on nutrition in context of ZHC

  – Coordinate members' support to SDG 2 and ZHC-related SDG goals and targets

  – Develop programmatic framework guidance to support and link joined-up regional and country action across five elements of ZHC, including elimination of stunting

 – Contribute, through CFS, to development of global norms

- *Accountability*

    – HLTF members are accountable to respective governing bodies; HLTF is chaired by the UN Secretary-General; Director-General FAO acts as executive Vice Chair and oversees independent HLTF coordination team

Enable timely, effective action for scaling up nutrition actions at country level, with focus on high-burden countries

- *Process/Institution*: Scaling Up Nutrition (SUN) movement – Coordination of UN system action through the UN Network for SUN (replacing the REACH Partnership), a joint secretariat supported by FAO, IFAD, UNICEF, WFP and WHO

- *Key responsibilities*:

    – Mobilize nutrition advocacy at all levels

    – Provide separate channels ("networks") for coordination of civil society, private sector, donor, and UN system support

    – Promote adoption of common results frameworks for monitoring and ensuring accountability for participating governments

    – Enable sharing of experiences and accumulation of best practices among SUN member-countries and partners

    – Promote partnerships with the private sector

- *Accountability*:

    – As a self-described "movement", SUN has no accountability to any UN intergovernmental body or process; it has a Lead Group appointed by the Secretary-General that provides high-level guidance, a Secretariat managed by the SUN Coordinator, and UN technical support from SCN and the participating agencies of the UN Network for SUN; countries and partners participate voluntarily; SUN places emphasis on making members accountable to citizens and partners for keeping commitments and resource mobilization

Specialized intergovernmental review of food security and nutrition issues can be provided by the Committee on World Food Security (CFS), which has a mandate to do so, although it has given limited attention to the full scope of nutrition issues in the past. Initially established to enable member-state oversight of inter-agency action in response to the food crisis of the early 1970s, the CFS was reformed in 2009 to incorporate two new features: an Advisory Group was established to enable the participation of non-state actors (among others, civil society organizations, private sector and producer organizations, non-governmental organizations, philanthropies, and policy experts) in the CFS policy deliberations; and a scientific advisory body, the High Level Panel of Experts (HLPE), was established to review the state of evidence and scientific thinking on key policy issues identified by the CFS in its periodically revised Multi-Year Programme of Work. Most of the staff and funding for the CFS Secretariat are provided by the three Rome-based agencies (RBAs): the Food and Agriculture Organization of the United Nations (FAO), the International Fund for Agriculture Development (IFAD), and the World Food Programme (WFP).

Today, the CFS is regarded by most experts as the state of the art in global-level multistakeholder platforms, giving voice to a wide variety of stakeholders and drawing on world-class scientific expertise, while also leaving the final decision-making to the UN member-states. According to sources closely involved in the CFS reform, the decision to limit non-state actors to an advisory role was strongly advocated by civil society as indispensable to ensuring member-state ownership of, and accountability for, CFS policy guidance and decisions (McKeon, 2014). It is the combination of structured access by non-state actors and ultimate member-state ownership that accounts for the unique success of the CFS framework.

A different type of multilateral framework frequently used in recent decades, and recommended in the ICN2 Rome Declaration, is the UN Decade of Action. The UN decades are often seen as boondoggles, expensive and practically useless publicity or advocacy exercises that are seldom supported by member-states, and which often deflect high-level attention away from established programme priorities. While there have been notorious failures in the past, more recent experience has shown that well-targeted decadal programmes of action, linked to widely shared developmental objectives, can help to catalyse intergovernmental cooperation, and even generate emulation and positive competition to improve results.

A UN Decade of Action on Nutrition for the years 2016–25 would serve at least two vital purposes. (1) It would help to provide a unified, cross-SDG focus on nutrition-related goals and targets within the new post-2015 development framework. This is needed to ensure the salience of nutrition as a key SDG objective in what is admittedly a crowded field but one that has enormous potential for broad, concerted action if there can be a mechanism to establish the necessary linkages among complementary actions.   (2) A UNGA declaration of such a decade would also ensure that the UN Secretariat receives the necessary directions to ensure adequate coordination of reporting, and to demonstrate credible commitment to harmonized or coordinated support at the global, regional, and country levels.

The costs of organizing and supporting a Decade of Action on Nutrition need not be great, given that the essential requirements are not for new institutions or resources for UN system coordination and support, but rather for adapting and better use of *existing* UN system supports. Three main mechanisms support the UN system action on nutrition: the UN Standing Committee on Nutrition (SCN), an inter-agency coordination mechanism established in 1977; the UN Secretary-General's High Level Task Force on Global Food Security and Nutrition (HLTF), which was formed in response to the food crises of 2008 and after; and the SUN movement.

Established as a follow-up action to the 1974 World Food Conference to "provide initiative in the development and harmonization of concepts, policies and strategies and programmes in the United Nations system in response to the nutritional needs of countries",[13] the SCN has long been a critical support to inter-agency policy coordination, and for many years provided one of the few sustained multistakeholder platforms for nutrition (Longhurst, 2010).   In recent years, it has been sharply criticized for not being able to adapt to changing circumstances and constitute itself as a mechanism for enabling sustained action at the country level; its multistakeholder platform, which featured non-governmental and civil society organizations but excluded private sector representatives, was also criticized as not conducive to the broader alliance that some organizations and several donors believe is critical to its success. The validity of such criticisms is disputed within the nutrition community, particularly in light of the current concerns about the need to establish robust firewalls around policy processes related to nutrition. Yet it is also clear that the SCN filled an important vacuum in enabling policy coordination among UN organizations and helped to sustain a nutrition focus across the UN system. It has a long-standing reporting relationship to the UN Economic and Social Council (EcoSoc), which had little practical significance in the recent past but which can play a vital role in the revamped SDG monitoring system that is currently being constructed by member-states.

The HLTF consists of twenty-two UN agencies, funds and programmes, as well as the Organization for Economic Cooperation and Development (OECD) and the World Trade Organization (WTO). It was initially formed to support advocacy and coordination of policy guidance among participating organizations, and produced a set of papers providing agreed policy

---

[13] UN EcoSoc (1977). See also UN EcoSoc (1976).

and programmatic guidance, including a Comprehensive Framework for Action that was twice revised. In 2013, the principals adopted new HLTF terms of reference that called for the reorganization of activity to support the Secretary-General's Zero Hunger Challenge (ZHC). The guiding vision of the ZHC, first declared by the Secretary-General in June 2012 at the United Nations Conference on Sustainable Development (known as Rio+20), is organized around five elements: 100 percent access to food at all times; zero stunting in children under 2 years of age; making all food systems sustainable; 100 percent increase in rural producers' productivity and income; and zero food loss and waste. These five elements are understood to be interdependent, and achievement of the Zero Hunger vision will require concerted action across a wide range of sectors. To highlight the centrality of nutrition objectives, HLTF members added the words "and Nutrition" to the official name of the HLTF in March 2015. Although never officially endorsed by the UNGA, the five elements of the Zero Hunger vision have been fully incorporated with modest amendment in the SDGs, four under the targets for SDG 2 and the fifth under SDG 12. The natural role of the HLTF is to build and coordinate broad international support for the Zero Hunger elements as they have become embedded in the new SDGs. The HLTF provides a natural bridge to a wider set of institutions with important, but limited, programmatic engagement in nutrition. The ZHC is also a convenient entry point for building alliances with broad social and political movements to end hunger, stop food loss and waste, and improve agricultural production and rural livelihoods sustainably.

During its first five years of existence, the SUN movement has demonstrated great power to build a broad alliance of international organizations committed to nutrition action. It has received strong endorsement from the nutritionist (specialist) community, and demonstrated a remarkable capacity for adaptation and innovation in its organizational structure and working procedures. The large number of country-members it has attracted is perhaps one of its most remarkable achievements. Yet, the SUN's own commissioned, independent, comprehensive evaluation concluded that the SUN movement had not yet been able to demonstrate systematic success in achieving its objective of scaling up nutrition action at the country level (Mokoro, 2015, p. 86.). This (early) result should not be surprising, given the powerful forces at work constraining effective nutrition action. But the limited effectiveness of SUN thus far does suggest the need for putting in place supports and institutional mechanisms that can sustain a global nutrition effort in the long run. It also reminds us why the SUN, constituted as a movement, cannot stand on its own as a central mechanism of global governance on nutrition. For nutrition advocacy the SUN has no peers, but it lacks the authority, legitimacy, and capacity for collective action that only governments, acting individually and collectively, can provide. And while the SUN's unique power comes from its distinctive character as a movement, it is not, as a movement, constituted to perform essential functions of governance: to prioritize choices, regulate behaviour in the public interest, allocate and commit resources, and accept accountability. The SUN is and will remain a vital pillar of a growing international architecture that supports a broad "system" of nutrition actors. But it is only one element of a growing ecosystem that depends vitally on a UN system that acts as the authoritative vehicle of collective action by nation-states.

Completing the reform

The core elements of a robust international system for nutrition are now in place, but several important adjustments are required. The SCN should be reformed, streamlining its functions by transferring its role as a multi-stakeholder platform to the CFS, and focusing more narrowly on supporting and sustaining global nutrition policy work. Key functions should include supporting inter-agency coordination and reporting on nutrition in the new SDGs; planning, coordinating, and sustaining a ten-year global plan of action as a follow-up to ICN2; and supporting formulation of UN positions on nutrition regulation through organs such as the CFS, WHA, and HLPF. SCN participation should be broadened to include the World Bank, among other major international organizations with strong nutrition programmes. The SCN should be sustained principally by contributions from participating institutions, which may be supplemented by UN member-states' contributions.

The CFS, which has an existing but, until recently, underserved mandate on nutrition, is expected to significantly expand its nutrition work in the coming years. The monitoring and reporting structures for the new SDGs have not yet been finalized, but it is clear already that the CFS is likely to play an important role in the expanded new framework for monitoring, analysing, and enabling political dialogue and action toward achieving the new SDGs. The UN Regional Commissions will also have a larger role, coordinating data collection and bottom-up monitoring and evaluation from the community, provincial, and national levels to the regional level.

Summing up, the proposed adaptation of the global architecture for nutrition governance builds on the coincidence of the launch of the new SDGs and the launch of a multi-year programme of action for nutrition to energize a broad, powerful, dynamic, and accountable member-state-owned system for enabling coordinated action at all levels. The reformed architecture also ensures compliance with intergovernmentally agreed norms and standards, including norms related to conflicts of interest, and provides for adequate and timely monitoring of outcomes and performance at all levels. It ensures a truly comprehensive and inclusive system for nutrition monitoring, and provides strong peer accountability for motivating effective action. It expands opportunities for meaningful participation of civil society and private sector organizations in the development of norms, standards, and policy guidance. By providing a universally relevant nutrition agenda that covers all three dimensions of malnutrition – undernourishment, micronutrient deficiencies, and obesity and other diet-related non-communicable diseases – it mainstreams nutrition concerns. Further, it secures nutrition as a principal driver for the full fifteen-year cycle of the next-generation global development agenda.

The critical test of this new, or for that matter any, institutional framework on nutrition is whether or not it contributes to overcoming the main sources of friction, fragmentation, and dissolution that have plagued nutrition actions in the past. The new nutrition architecture addresses several of these issues by ensuring that a comprehensive nutrition agenda will be constantly measured and monitored. Governments are more likely to be compelled by the pressure on their reputations that comes from constant reporting of successes and failures, than by the always limited political pressure of accountability to the poor and vulnerable who constitute the majority of those suffering most from all aspects of undernutrition. While the new architecture cannot guarantee the mobilization of adequate human and financial resources, it does ensure that commitment and support for nutrition will be prolonged and relentless. If it is fully energized by a declared decade of coordinated action, the architecture can make the UN system achieve its nutrition goals. But for that to happen, changes are required in the way the UN perceives and executes its own role in enabling an ecosystem of actors and institutions to flourish.

Recasting the UN's role

Thus far we have directed our discussion to the key role that multilateral institutions can play in establishing a milieu for sustained effective action on nutrition. This should not lead us to expect that such an enabling environment can be supplied by the UN system alone. The material, scientific, technical, organizational, educational, political, technological, and financial resources to address malnutrition are far beyond the resources of UN agencies, funds, and programmes. Still, the UN has a vital and unique role to play as an enabler of others' actions in this field.

The UN has impressive, if not always well-utilized, capacity to facilitate others' policy actions. For example, by enabling the development and promulgation of regulations for food safety through institutions such as the Codex Alimentarius, the international food standards body jointly supported by the FAO and WHO, the UN can influence private business practices and encourage innovation in food products and services, including food storage and handling, reductions in food loss and waste, and improvements in the nutritional quality of commercial food products. Developing and improving a food systems approach to nutrition, as advocated in the ICN2 Framework for Action, is inconceivable unless the agenda is fully accepted by the private sector as essential to its own long-term health and prosperity. The UN has an important role to play in supporting the member-states' efforts to develop rules and regulations for an appropriate enabling environment for the functioning of food systems for nutrition. Similarly, while the UN cannot claim to be a leading global centre for research on nutrition, it has an important role to play in bringing the best experience and research to the attention of key policymakers to whom it has privileged access under its own auspices.

Because many different kinds of social actors are required to accelerate momentum on nutrition action, it is frequently argued, erroneously in our view, that UN institutions should take a more limited view of their role and accept a position as one of many equal partners in development, with no more right to claim priority for their views than any other institution. The same line of thinking leads to a *laissez faire* or "anything goes" attitude toward partnerships; we need action, it is often said, and we don't have time for UN deliberations to decide what needs to be done. Let those who can, and want to, contribute do so, and let the beneficiary countries decide what is most helpful for them.

Such views, to a large extent, are misguided. If widely adopted, they will sooner than later undermine the potential for genuine multistakeholder partnership that exists in many areas of nutrition action today. They will undermine confidence that these partnerships are guided by a genuine public interest. They will also undermine it by limiting what is put on offer to what the providers themselves want to offer; which leads to a reduced set of choices and an impoverished dialogue between development partners and their beneficiaries. Finally, such misguided views will discourage UN bodies from playing important regulatory and governance roles that only legitimate multilateral organizations can play to establish effective cooperation among the vast array of institutions involved in nutrition today.

Today, a heated debate surrounds the role of alliances or partnerships with the private sector and other non-state actors in achieving development outcomes. In the area of nutrition, four issues stand out. First, how are these non-state actors to be made accountable to the host or beneficiary nations? The current vogue is for promoting beneficiary country accountability to international actors – donors, CSOs and NGOs, and private sector entities – but not the other way round. Mutual accountability, the catch-phrase of international political correctness, has little practical meaning in these contexts. Too often, the effort is to make the recipient country's processes and expenditures fully transparent, but reporting by intentional actors, if it exists at all, to host governments is comparatively limited. In such circumstances, the international presence also works to undermine governmental authority and capacity by establishing institutions that operate parallel to local and even national governments, and compete with them for resources and talent.

Secondly, the question of how to engage with the private sector is particularly acute. Given the well-known history of interference in national and international regulatory bodies, there is a need for strong and credible protections against conflicts of interest, but few public–private partnerships take this responsibility seriously, and action on this front is usually limited to a memorandum of understanding without practical or legal effect, and with limited, if any, investment in monitoring and enforcement. In the context of the extreme asymmetries of power, information, and resources that exist between many developing countries and large multinational corporations, there is clear need for a neutral third party to help define – and monitor and enforce – the clear rules of the game. This is in the best interests of both the developing countries and the large corporate entities, who need help with setting the boundaries of acceptable behaviour where individuals from both the private and public sides too easily pursue private ends that undermine public policy and trust in public institutions.

A third area of contention surrounds the need for enabling developing countries' governments to play a meaningful role in deciding what policy objectives and means of support should be prioritized. The private sector and non-state actors are less likely to offer what developing countries need if decisions are all made on the supply side; intergovernmental processes where donors and beneficiaries meet to assess needs offer the most balanced, if not always satisfying, forums for defining and matching needs and responses, developing appropriate policy guidance, and mobilizing financial and other means of implementation.

Finally, there is the matter of accountability. Developing countries complain that efforts to shift the discussion of development partnership from intergovernmental processes to public–private partnerships lead to much weaker forms of mutual accountability than the admittedly challenged multilateral processes. Intergovernmental forums, and the agreements produced in them, typically lead to institutionalized monitoring and reporting of follow-up actions, unlike pledges, memoranda of understanding, and other such transactions with non-state actors. Private sector investment pledges are seldom followed through, and there is, in any case, rarely any mechanism for follow-up tracking and reporting.

To address these issues, there are at least four important functions and roles that UN institutions are uniquely called on to play at regional and country levels, which cannot be played by other international actors either at all or as well: (1) developing – and monitoring and ensuring compliance with – intergovernmentally agreed norms, including voluntary guidelines and conflict of interest rules; (2) providing a critical but informed forum for discussion of key policy issues and development of internationally agreed guidance, enabling mutual learning, often through South–South cooperation; (3) providing global data standards to enable consistent and comparable monitoring of progress; and (4) serving as a neutral broker for information and expertise. The unique status of UN institutions in their accountability to the member-states is decisive for enabling the UN to fulfil each of these functions.

To be truly effective in enabling action by others, each of these functions must be performed so that they are trusted not only by host governments, but also by the vast array of international partners offering their own services and supports. But here lies a dilemma. For all UN institutions, establishing and maintaining an important ground presence requires reliance not only on the goodwill of host governments, but also on the support of public and, increasingly, private donors. To this extent, multilateral institutions inevitably find themselves in a competitive situation with the other actors whose nutrition actions they hope to regulate through moral suasion, and with one another. To this extent, they stand as one more donor supplicant in the highly competitive "aid industry".

What can be done to preserve the integrity of multilateral institutions and ensure that their country-level presence is genuinely guided by the interests of the host government? The answer is disarmingly simple: ensure accountability through an intergovernmental process. In the end, this is what distinguishes true multilateral partnership from other forms of partnership based principally on like-mindedness, mutual interest or mere convenience. The reason that accountability to an intergovernmental process matters is that it is so far the only reliable guarantee for a developing country to ensure that it can freely decide, albeit in often complex and challenging circumstances, a course for itself. The outcomes of multilateral processes are full of compromises. But they are the most reasonable outcomes attainable for enabling countries to plot their own development pathways. Multilateral processes are time-consuming and difficult precisely because much is at stake, particularly for the developing countries. Put simply, it is in a multilateral system that developing countries have a real say and where they feel an obligation to comply with agreed commitments. That is why the temptation to bypass such processes will possibly lead to occasional short-term successes, but also, more often than not, to general failure.

An effective system for governance of global nutrition action must be deeply rooted in the norms, member-state agreements, and institutional architecture of the UN system.

Appendix A

ICN2: Rome Declaration on Nutrition

Second International Conference on Nutrition
Rome, 19–21 November 2014
Conference Outcome Document: Rome Declaration on Nutrition

Welcoming the participation of Heads of State and Government and other high-level guests,

1. We, Ministers and Representatives of the Members of the Food and Agriculture Organization of the United Nations (FAO) and the World Health Organization (WHO), assembled at the Second International Conference on Nutrition in Rome from 19 to 21 November 2014, jointly organized by FAO and WHO, to address the multiple challenges of malnutrition in all its forms and identify opportunities for tackling them in the next decades.

2. Reaffirming the commitments made at the first International Conference on Nutrition in 1992, and the World Food Summits in 1996 and 2002 and the World Summit on Food Security in 2009, as well as in relevant international targets and action plans, including the WHO 2025 Global Nutrition Targets and the WHO Global Action Plan for the Prevention and Control of Noncommunicable Diseases 2013-2020.

3. Reaffirming the right of everyone to have access to safe, sufficient, and nutritious food, consistent with the right to adequate food and the fundamental right of everyone to be free from hunger consistent with the International Covenant on Economic, Social and Cultural Rights and other relevant United Nations instruments.

Multiple challenges of malnutrition to inclusive and sustainable development and to health

4. Acknowledge that malnutrition, in all its forms, including under-nutrition, micronutrient deficiencies, overweight and obesity, not only affects people's health and wellbeing by impacting negatively on human physical and cognitive development, compromising the immune system, increasing susceptibility to communicable and non-communicable diseases, restricting the attainment of human potential and reducing productivity, but also poses a high burden in the form of negative social and economic consequences to individuals, families, communities and States.

5. Recognize that the root causes of and factors leading to malnutrition are complex and multidimensional:

   a) poverty, underdevelopment and low socio-economic status are major contributors to malnutrition in both rural and urban areas;

   b) the lack of access at all times to sufficient food, which is adequate both in quantity and quality which conforms with the beliefs, culture, traditions, dietary habits and preferences of individuals in accordance with national and international laws and obligations;

   c) malnutrition is often aggravated by poor infant and young child feeding and care practices, poor sanitation and hygiene, lack of access to education, quality health systems and safe drinking water, foodborne infections and parasitic infestations, ingestion of harmful levels of contaminants due to unsafe food from production to consumption;

   d) epidemics, such as of the Ebola virus disease, pose tremendous challenges to food security and nutrition.

6. Acknowledge that different forms of malnutrition co-exist within most countries; while dietary risk affects all socio-economic groups, large inequalities exist in nutritional status, exposure to risk and adequacy of dietary energy and nutrient intake, between and within countries.

7. Recognize that some socioeconomic and environmental changes can have an impact on dietary and physical activity patterns, leading to higher susceptibility to obesity and noncommunicable diseases through increasing sedentary lifestyles and consumption of food that is high in fat, especially saturated and trans-fats, sugars, and salt/sodium.

8. Recognize the need to address the impacts of climate change and other environmental factors on food security and nutrition, in particular on the quantity, quality and diversity of food produced, taking appropriate action to tackle negative effects.

9. Recognize that conflict and post conflict situations, humanitarian emergencies and protracted crises, including, *inter alia*, droughts, floods and desertification as well as pandemics, hinder food security and nutrition.

10. Acknowledge that current food systems are being increasingly challenged to provide adequate, safe, diversified and nutrient rich food for all that contribute to healthy diets due to, inter alia, constraints posed by resource scarcity and environmental degradation, as well as by unsustainable production and consumption patterns, food losses and waste, and unbalanced distribution.

11. Acknowledge that trade is a key element in achieving food security and nutrition and that trade policies are to be conducive to fostering food security and nutrition for all, through a fair and market-oriented world trade system, and reaffirm the need to refrain from unilateral measures not in accordance with international law, including the Charter of the United Nations, and which endanger food security and nutrition, as stated in the 1996 Rome Declaration.

12. Note with profound concern that, notwithstanding significant achievements in many countries, recent decades have seen modest and uneven progress in reducing malnutrition and estimated figures show that:

   a) the prevalence of undernourishment has moderately declined, but absolute numbers remain unacceptably high with an estimated 805 million people suffering chronically from hunger in 2012–2014;

   b) chronic malnutrition as measured by stunting has declined, but in 2013 still affected 161 million children under five years of age, while acute malnutrition (wasting) affected 51 million children under five years of age;

   c) undernutrition was the main underlying cause of death in children under five, causing 45% of all child deaths in the world in 2013;

   d) over two billion people suffer from micronutrient deficiencies, in particular vitamin A, iodine, iron and zinc, among others;

e) overweight and obesity among both children and adults have been increasing rapidly in all regions, with 42 million children under five years of age affected by overweight in 2013 and over 500 million adults affected by obesity in 2010;

f) dietary risk factors, together with inadequate physical activity, account for almost 10% of the global burden of disease and disability.

A common vision for global action to end all forms of malnutrition

13. We reaffirm that:

a) the elimination of malnutrition in all its forms is an imperative for health, ethical, political, social and economic reasons, paying particular attention to the special needs of children, women, the elderly, persons with disabilities, other vulnerable groups as well as people in humanitarian emergencies;

b) nutrition policies should promote a diversified, balanced and healthy diet at all stages of life. In particular, special attention should be given to the first 1,000 days, from the start of pregnancy to two years of age, pregnant and lactating women, women of reproductive age, and adolescent girls, by promoting and supporting adequate care and feeding practices, including exclusive breast feeding during the first six months, and continued breastfeeding until two years of age and beyond with appropriate complementary feeding. Healthy diets should be fostered in preschools, schools, public institutions, at the workplace and at home, as well as healthy eating by families;

c) coordinated action among different actors, across all relevant sectors at international, regional, national and community levels, needs to be supported through cross-cutting and coherent policies, programmes and initiatives, including social protection, to address the multiple burdens of malnutrition and to promote sustainable food systems;

d) food should not be used as an instrument for political or economic pressure;

e) excessive volatility of prices of food and agricultural commodities can negatively impact food security and nutrition, and needs to be better monitored and addressed for the challenges it poses;

f) improvements in diet and nutrition require relevant legislative frameworks for food safety and quality, including for the proper use of agrochemicals, by promoting participation in the activities of the Codex Alimentarius Commission for the development of international standards for food safety and quality, as well as for improving information for consumers, while avoiding inappropriate marketing and publicity of foods and non-alcoholic beverages to children, as recommended by resolution WHA63.14;

g) nutrition data and indicators, as well as the capacity of, and support to all countries, especially developing countries, for data collection and analysis, need to be improved in order to contribute to more effective nutrition surveillance, policy making and accountability;

h) empowerment of consumers is necessary through improved and evidence-based health and nutrition information and education to make informed choices regarding consumption of food products for healthy dietary practices;

i) national health systems should integrate nutrition while providing access for all to integrated health services through a continuum of care approach, including health promotion and disease prevention, treatment and rehabilitation, and contribute to reducing inequalities through addressing specific nutrition-related needs and vulnerabilities of different population groups;

j) nutrition and other related policies should pay special attention to women and empower women and girls, thereby contributing to women's full and equal access to social protection and resources, including, *inter alia*, income, land, water, finance, education, training, science and technology, and health services, thus promoting food security and health.

14. We recognize that:

a) international cooperation and Official Development Assistance for nutrition should support and complement national nutrition strategies, policies and programmes, and surveillance initiatives, as appropriate;

b) the progressive realization of the right to adequate food in the context of national food security is fostered through sustainable, equitable, accessible in all cases, and resilient and diverse food systems;

c) collective action is instrumental to improve nutrition, requiring collaboration between governments, the private sector, civil society and communities;

d) non-discriminatory and secure access and utilization of resources in accordance with international law are important for food security and nutrition;

e) food and agriculture systems, including crops, livestock, forestry, fisheries and aquaculture, need to be addressed comprehensively through coordinated public policies, taking into account the resources, investment, environment, people, institutions and processes with which food is produced, processed, stored, distributed, prepared and consumed;

f) family farmers and small holders, notably women farmers, play an important role in reducing malnutrition and should be supported by integrated and multisectoral public policies, as appropriate, that raise their productive capacity and incomes and strengthen their resilience;

g) wars, occupations, terrorism, civil disturbances and natural disasters, disease outbreaks and epidemics, as well as human rights violations and inappropriate socio-economic policies, have resulted in tens of millions of refugees, displaced persons, war affected non-combatant civilian populations and migrants, who are among the most nutritionally vulnerable groups. Resources for rehabilitating and caring for these groups are often extremely inadequate and nutritional deficiencies are common. All responsible parties should cooperate to ensure the safe and timely passage and distribution of food and medical supplies to those in need, which conforms with the beliefs, culture, traditions, dietary habits and preferences of individuals, in accordance with national legislation and international law and obligations and the Charter of the United Nations;

h) responsible investment in agriculture[1], including small holders and family farming and in food systems, is essential for overcoming malnutrition;

i) governments should protect consumers, especially children, from inappropriate marketing and publicity of food;

j) nutrition improvement requires healthy, balanced, diversified diets, including traditional diets where appropriate, meeting nutrient requirements of all age groups, and all groups with special nutrition needs, while avoiding the excessive intake of saturated fat, sugars and salt/sodium, and virtually eliminating trans-fat, among others;

---

[1] The term agriculture includes crops, livestock, forestry and fisheries.

k) food systems should provide year-round access to foods that cover people's nutrient needs and promote healthy dietary practices;

l) food systems need to contribute to preventing and addressing infectious diseases, including zoonotic diseases, and tackling antimicrobial resistance;

m) food systems, including all components of production, processing and distribution should be sustainable, resilient and efficient in providing more diverse foods in an equitable manner, with due attention to assessing environmental and health impacts;

n) food losses and waste throughout the food chain should be reduced in order to contribute to food security, nutrition, and sustainable development;

o) the United Nations system, including the Committee on World Food Security, and international and regional financial institutions should work more effectively together in order to support national and regional efforts, as appropriate, and enhance international cooperation and development assistance to accelerate progress in addressing malnutrition;

p) EXPO MILANO 2015, dedicated to "feeding the planet, energy for life", among other relevant events and fora, will provide an opportunity to stress the importance of food security and nutrition, raise public awareness, foster debate, and give visibility to the ICN2 outcomes.

Commitment to action

15. We commit to:

a) eradicate hunger and prevent all forms of malnutrition worldwide, particularly undernourishment, stunting, wasting, underweight and overweight in children under five years of age; and anaemia in women and children among other micronutrient deficiencies; as well as reverse the rising trends in overweight and obesity and reduce the burden of diet-related noncommunicable diseases in all age groups;

b) increase investments for effective interventions and actions to improve people's diets and nutrition, including in emergency situations;

c) enhance sustainable food systems by developing coherent public policies from production to consumption and across relevant sectors to provide year-round access to food that meets people's nutrition needs and promote safe and diversified healthy diets;

d) raise the profile of nutrition within relevant national strategies, policies, actions plans and programmes, and align national resources accordingly;

e) improve nutrition by strengthening human and institutional capacities to address all forms of malnutrition through, inter alia, relevant scientific and socio-economic research and development, innovation and transfer of appropriate technologies on mutually agreed terms and conditions;

f) strengthen and facilitate contributions and action by all stakeholders to improve nutrition and promote collaboration within and across countries, including North–South cooperation, as well as South–South and triangular cooperation;

g) develop policies, programmes and initiatives for ensuring healthy diets throughout the life course, starting from the early stages of life to adulthood, including of people with special nutritional needs, before and during pregnancy, in particular during the first 1,000 days, promoting, protecting and supporting exclusive breastfeeding during the first six months and continued breastfeeding until two years of age and beyond with appropriate complementary feeding, healthy eating by families, and at school during childhood, as well as other specialized feeding;

h) empower people and create an enabling environment for making informed choices about food products for healthy dietary practices and appropriate infant and young child feeding practices through improved health and nutrition information and education;

i) implement the commitments of this Declaration through the Framework for Action which will also contribute to ensuring accountability and monitoring progress in global nutrition targets;

j) give due consideration to integrating the vision and commitments of this Declaration into the post-2015 development agenda process including a possible related global goal.

16. We call on FAO and WHO, in collaboration with other United Nations agencies, funds and programmes, as well as other international organizations, to support national governments, upon request, in developing, strengthening and implementing their policies, programmes and plans to address the multiple challenges of malnutrition.

17. We recommend to the United Nations General Assembly to endorse the Rome Declaration on Nutrition, as well as the Framework for Action which provides a set of voluntary policy options and strategies

for use by governments, as appropriate, and to consider declaring a Decade of Action on Nutrition from 2016 to 2025 within existing structures and available resources.

Appendix B

ICN2: Framework for Action

Second International Conference on Nutrition
Rome, 19–21 November 2014
Conference Outcome Document: Framework for Action

FROM COMMITMENTS TO ACTION

Background

1. There has been a significant improvement in reducing hunger and malnutrition of the world's population since the 1992 International Conference on Nutrition (ICN). Yet, progress in reducing hunger and undernutrition has been uneven and unacceptably slow. The fundamental challenge today is to sustainably improve nutrition through implementation of coherent policies and better coordinated actions across all relevant sectors.

Purpose and targets

2. The nature of this Framework for Action is voluntary. Its purpose is to guide the implementation of the commitments of the Rome Declaration on Nutrition adopted by the Second International Conference on Nutrition held in Rome, Italy, on 19–21 November 2014. Building on existing commitments, goals and targets, this Framework for Action provides a set of policy options and strategies which governments[1], acting in cooperation with other stakeholders, may incorporate, as appropriate, into their national nutrition, health, agriculture[2], development and investment plans, and consider in

---

[1] The term 'governments' is understood to include the European Union and other regional organizations on matters of their competency.
[2] In this document, the term 'agriculture' comprises crops, livestock, forestry and fisheries.

negotiating international agreements to achieve better nutrition for all.

3. As governments have primary responsibility for taking action at country level, in dialogue with a wide range of stakeholders, including affected communities, the recommendations are principally addressed to government leaders. They will consider the appropriateness of the recommended policies and actions in relation to national needs and conditions, as well as regional and national priorities, including in legal frameworks. For the purpose of accountability, this Framework for Action adopts existing global targets for improving maternal, infant and young child nutrition[3] and for noncommunicable disease risk factor reduction[4] to be achieved by 2025.

Recommended set of policy and programme options

4. The following set of policy and programme options are recommended to create an enabling environment and to improve nutrition in all sectors.

Recommended actions to create an enabling environment for effective action

- Recommendation 1: Enhance political commitment and social participation for improving nutrition at the country level through political dialogue and advocacy.

- Recommendation 2: Develop – or revise, as appropriate – and cost National Nutrition Plans, align policies that impact nutrition across different ministries and agencies, and strengthen legal frameworks and strategic capacities for nutrition.

- Recommendation 3: Strengthen and establish, as appropriate, national cross-government, inter- sector, multi-stakeholder mechanisms for food security and nutrition to oversee implementation of policies, strategies, programmes and other investments in nutrition. Such platforms may be needed at various levels, with robust safeguards against abuse and conflicts of interest.

---

[3] Namely: (1) 40% reduction of the global number of children under five who are stunted; (2) 50% reduction of anaemia in women of reproductive age; (3) 30% reduction of low birth weight; (4) no increase in childhood overweight; (5) increase exclusive breastfeeding rates in the first six months up to at least 50%; and (6) reduce and maintain childhood wasting to less than 5%.

[4] Namely: (1) to reduce salt intake by 30%; and (2) to halt the increase in obesity prevalence in adolescents and adults.

- Recommendation 4: Increase responsible and sustainable investment in nutrition, especially at country level with domestic finance; generate additional resources through innovative financing tools; engage development partners to increase Official Development Assistance in nutrition and foster private investments as appropriate.

- Recommendation 5: Improve the availability, quality, quantity, coverage and management of multisectoral information systems related to food and nutrition for improved policy development and accountability.

- Recommendation 6: Promote inter-country collaboration, such as North–South, South–South and triangular cooperation, and information exchange on nutrition, food, technology, research, policies and programmes.

- Recommendation 7: Strengthen nutrition governance and coordinate policies, strategies and programmes of United Nations system agencies, programmes and funds within their respective mandates.

Recommended actions for sustainable food systems promoting healthy diets

- Recommendation 8: Review national policies and investments and integrate nutrition objectives into food and agriculture policy, programme design and implementation, to enhance nutrition sensitive agriculture, ensure food security and enable healthy diets.

- Recommendation 9: Strengthen local food production and processing, especially by smallholder[5] and family farmers, giving special attention to women's empowerment, while recognizing that efficient and effective trade is key to achieving nutrition objectives.

- Recommendation 10: Promote the diversification of crops including underutilized traditional crops, more production of fruits and vegetables, and appropriate production of animal-source products as needed, applying sustainable food production and natural resource management practices.

- Recommendation 11: Improve storage, preservation, transport and distribution technologies and infrastructure to reduce seasonal food insecurity, food and nutrient loss and waste.

---

[5] Smallholder farmers include agriculture and food workers, artisanal fisherfolk, pastoralists, indigenous peoples and the landless (Committee on World Food Security, Global Strategic Framework for Food Security and Nutrition, 2013).

- Recommendation 12: Establish and strengthen institutions, policies, programmes and services to enhance the resilience of the food supply in crisis-prone areas, including areas affected by climate change.

- Recommendation 13: Develop, adopt and adapt, where appropriate, international guidelines on healthy diets.

- Recommendation 14: Encourage gradual reduction of saturated fat, sugars and salt/sodium and trans-fat from foods and beverages to prevent excessive intake by consumers and improve nutrient content of foods, as needed.

- Recommendation 15: Explore regulatory and voluntary instruments – such as marketing, publicity and labelling policies, economic incentives or disincentives in accordance with Codex Alimentarius and World Trade Organization rules – to promote healthy diets.

- Recommendation 16: Establish food or nutrient-based standards to make healthy diets and safe drinking water accessible in public facilities such as hospitals, childcare facilities, workplaces, universities, schools, food and catering services, government offices and prisons, and encourage the establishment of facilities for breastfeeding.

Recommended actions in international trade and investment

- Recommendation 17: Encourage governments, United Nations agencies, programmes and funds, the World Trade Organization and other international organizations to identify opportunities to achieve global food and nutrition targets, through trade and investment policies.

- Recommendation 18: Improve the availability and access of the food supply through appropriate trade agreements and policies and endeavour to ensure that such agreements and policies do not have a negative impact on the right to adequate food in other countries[6].

Recommended actions for nutrition education and information

- Recommendation 19: Implement nutrition education and information interventions based on national dietary guidelines and coherent policies related to food and diets, through improved school curricula, nutrition education in the health, agriculture and social protection services, community interventions and point-of-sale information, including labelling.

---

[6] United Nations General Assembly resolution A/RES/68/177, paragraph 25.

- Recommendation 20: Build nutrition skills and capacity to undertake nutrition education activities, particularly for front line workers, social workers, agricultural extension personnel, teachers and health professionals.

- Recommendation 21: Conduct appropriate social marketing campaigns and lifestyle change communication programmes to promote physical activity, dietary diversification, consumption of micronutrient-rich foods such as fruits and vegetables, including traditional local foods and taking into consideration cultural aspects, better child and maternal nutrition, appropriate care practices and adequate breastfeeding and complementary feeding, targeted and adapted for different audiences and stakeholders in the food system.

Recommended actions on social protection

- Recommendation 22: Incorporate nutrition objectives into social protection programmes and into humanitarian assistance safety net programmes.

- Recommendation 23: Use cash and food transfers, including school feeding programmes and other forms of social protection for vulnerable populations to improve diets through better access to food which conforms with the beliefs, culture, traditions, dietary habits and preferences of individuals in accordance with national and international laws and obligations, and which is nutritionally adequate for healthy diets.

- Recommendation 24: Increase income for the most vulnerable populations by creating decent jobs for all, including through the promotion of self-employment.

Recommended actions for strong and resilient health systems

- Recommendation 25: Strengthen health systems and promote universal health coverage[7], particularly through primary health care, to enable national health systems to address malnutrition in all its forms.

---

[7] In accordance with preambular paragraph 9 of resolution WHA67.14, universal health coverage implies that all people have access without discrimination to nationally determined sets of the needed promotive, preventive, curative, palliative and rehabilitative essential health services and essential, safe, affordable, effective and quality medicines, while ensuring that the use of these services does not expose the users to financial hardship with a special emphasis on the poor, vulnerable and marginalized segments of the population.

- Recommendation 26: Improve the integration of nutrition actions into health systems through appropriate strategies for strengthening human resources, leadership and governance, health system financing and service delivery, as well as the provision of essential medicines, information and monitoring.

- Recommendation 27: Promote universal access to all direct nutrition actions and relevant health actions impacting nutrition through health programmes.

- Recommendation 28: Implement the WHO Global Strategy on Infant and Young Child Feeding, the WHO Comprehensive Implementation Plan on Maternal, Infant and Young Child Nutrition 2012–2025, and the WHO Global Action Plan for the Prevention and Control of Noncommunicable Diseases 2013–2020 through commensurate financing and adequate policies.

Recommended actions to promote, protect and support breastfeeding

- Recommendation 29: Adapt and implement the International Code of Marketing of Breast-milk Substitutes and subsequent relevant World Health Assembly resolutions.

- Recommendation 30: Implement policies and practices, including labour reforms, as appropriate, to promote protection of working mothers[8].

- Recommendation 31: Implement policies, programmes and actions to ensure that health services promote, protect and support breastfeeding, including the Baby-Friendly Hospital Initiative.

- Recommendation 32: Encourage and promote – through advocacy, education and capacity building – an enabling environment where men, particularly fathers, participate actively and share responsibilities with mothers in caring for their infants and young children, while empowering women and enhancing their health and nutritional status throughout the life course.

- Recommendation 33: Ensure that policies and practices in emergency situations and humanitarian crises promote, protect and support breastfeeding.

---

[8] As specified in the International Labour Organization's Maternity Protection Convention No. 183 and corresponding Recommendation 191.

Recommended actions to address wasting

- Recommendation 34: Adopt policies and actions, and mobilize funding, to improve coverage of treatment for wasting, using the community-based management of acute malnutrition approach and improve the integrated management of childhood illnesses.

- Recommendation 35: Integrate disaster and emergency preparedness into relevant policies and programmes.

Recommended actions to address stunting

- Recommendation 36: Establish policies and strengthen interventions to improve maternal nutrition and health, beginning with adolescent girls and continuing through pregnancy and lactation.

- Recommendation 37: Establish health policies, programmes and strategies to promote optimal infant and young child feeding, particularly exclusive breastfeeding up to six months, followed by adequate complementary feeding (from six to 24 months).

Recommended actions to address childhood overweight and obesity

- Recommendation 38: Provide dietary counselling to women during pregnancy for healthy weight gain and adequate nutrition.

- Recommendation 39: Improve child nutritional status and growth, particularly by addressing maternal exposure to the availability and marketing of complementary foods, and by improving supplementary feeding programmes for infants and young children.

- Recommendation 40: Regulate the marketing of food and non-alcoholic beverages to children in accordance with WHO recommendations.

- Recommendation 41: Create a conducive environment that promotes physical activity to address sedentary lifestyle from the early stages of life.

Recommended actions to address anaemia in women of reproductive age

- Recommendation 42: Improve intake of micronutrients through consumption of nutrient-dense foods, especially foods rich in iron, where necessary, through fortification and supplementation strategies, and promote healthy and diversified diets.

- Recommendation 43: Provide daily iron and folic acid and other micronutrient supplementation to pregnant women as part of antenatal care; and intermittent iron and folic acid supplementation to menstruating women where the prevalence of anaemia is 20% or higher, and deworming, where appropriate.

Recommended actions in the health services to improve nutrition

- Recommendation 44: Implement policies and programmes to ensure universal access to and use of insecticide-treated nets, and to provide preventive malaria treatment for pregnant women in areas with moderate to high malaria transmission.

- Recommendation 45: Provide periodic deworming for all school-age children in endemic areas.

- Recommendation 46: Implement policies and programmes to improve health service capacity to prevent and treat infectious diseases[9].

- Recommendation 47: Provide zinc supplementation to reduce the duration and severity of diarrhoea, and to prevent subsequent episodes in children.

- Recommendation 48: Provide iron and, among others, vitamin A supplementation for pre-school children to reduce the risk of anaemia.

- Recommendation 49: Implement policies and strategies to ensure that women have comprehensive information and access to integral health care services that ensure adequate support for safe pregnancy and delivery.

Recommended actions on water, sanitation and hygiene

- Recommendation 50: Implement policies and programmes using participatory approaches to improve water management in agriculture and food production.[10]

- Recommendation 51: Invest in and commit to achieve universal access to safe drinking water, with the participation of civil society and the support of international partners, as appropriate.

---

[9] Including prevention of mother-to-child transmission of HIV, immunization against measles and antibiotic treatment for girls with urinary infections.
[10] Including by reducing water wastage in irrigation, strategies for multiple use of water (including wastewater), and better use of appropriate technology.

- Recommendation 52: Implement policies and strategies using participatory approaches to ensure universal access to adequate sanitation[11] and to promote safe hygiene practices, including hand washing with soap.

Recommended actions on food safety and antimicrobial resistance

- Recommendation 53: Develop, establish, enforce and strengthen, as appropriate, food control systems, including reviewing and modernizing national food safety legislation and regulations to ensure that food producers and suppliers throughout the food chain operate responsibly.

- Recommendation 54: Actively take part in the work of the Codex Alimentarius Commission on nutrition and food safety, and implement, as appropriate, internationally adopted standards at the national level.

- Recommendation 55: Participate in and contribute to international networks to exchange food safety information, including for managing emergencies[12].

- Recommendation 56: Raise awareness among relevant stakeholders on the problems posed by antimicrobial resistance, and implement appropriate multisectoral measures to address antimicrobial resistance, including prudent use of antimicrobials in veterinary and human medicine.

- Recommendation 57: Develop and implement national guidelines on prudent use of antimicrobials in food-producing animals according to internationally recognized standards adopted by competent international organizations to reduce non-therapeutic use of antimicrobials and to phase out the use of antimicrobials as growth promoters in the absence of risk analysis as described in Codex Code of Practice CAC/RCP61-2005.

Recommendations for accountability

- Recommendation 58: National governments are encouraged to establish nutrition targets and intermediate milestones, consistent with the timeframe for implementation (2016–2025), as well as global nutrition and noncommunicable disease targets established by the

---

[11] Including by implementing effective risk assessment and management practices on safe wastewater use and sanitation.

[12] FAO/WHO International Network of Food Safety Authorities (http://www.who.int/foodsafety/areas_work/infosan/en/).

World Health Assembly. They are invited to include – in their national monitoring frameworks – agreed international indicators for nutrition outcomes (to track progress in achieving national targets), nutrition programme implementation (including coverage of interventions) and the nutrition policy environment (including institutional arrangements, capacities and investments in nutrition)[13]. Monitoring should be conducted, to the fullest possible extent, through existing mechanisms.

- Recommendation 59: Reports on implementation of the commitments of the Rome Declaration on Nutrition will be compiled jointly by FAO and WHO, in close collaboration with other United Nations agencies, funds and programmes and other relevant regional and international organizations, as appropriate, based on country self-assessments as well as information available through other monitoring and accountability mechanisms (e.g. Scaling Up Nutrition self-assessment reports, reports to the FAO Conference and the World Health Assembly, and the Global Nutrition Report).

- Recommendation 60: The governing bodies of FAO and WHO, and other relevant international organizations are requested to consider the inclusion of reports on the overall follow-up to ICN2 on the agendas of the regular FAO and WHO governing body meetings, including FAO regional conferences and WHO regional committee meetings, possibly on a biennial basis. The Directors-General of FAO and WHO are also requested to transmit such reports to the United Nations General Assembly as appropriate.

---

[13] Monitoring frameworks may be developed based on the Global Monitoring Framework for Maternal, Infant and Young Child Nutrition, the Monitoring Framework for the Global Action Plan on Noncommunicable Diseases, as well as indicatorsfor monitoring food security (FAO prevalence of undernutrition, food insecurity experience scale, and other widely used indicators).

Appendix C

ICN2: Information Note on the Framework for Action

Joint FAO–WHO ICN2 Secretariat
4 November 2014

> ### Summary: Key Messages from the Framework for Action
>
> - For effective implementation of policies to improve nutrition an **enabling policy environment** is essential. This means explicit political commitment, greater investment, cross-government policies and plans, along with multi-stakeholder governance mechanisms.
>
> - **Sustainable food systems** are key to promoting healthy diets, and innovative food system solutions are needed.
>
> - Information and education concerning healthy dietary practices are vital, but consumers must also be empowered through enabling **food environments** that provide safe, diverse and healthy diets.
>
> - While a food systems approach is important, **coherent action** is also needed in other sectors. These include international trade and investment, nutrition education and information, social protection, health system delivery of direct nutrition interventions and other health services to promote nutrition, water, sanitation and hygiene, and food safety.
>
> - For the purpose of **accountability**, the Framework for Action adopts existing global targets for improving maternal, infant and young child nutrition and for noncommunicable disease (NCD) risk factor reduction.

1. INTRODUCTION

The political declaration of the Second International Conference on Nutrition to be held in Rome, Italy, on 19–21 November 2014 addresses the multiple challenges of malnutrition in all its forms to inclusive and sustainable development and health. The 10 commitments of the Rome Declaration on Nutrition (see box) set out a common vision and provide a mandate, as well as the obligations, for governments to address nutrition in the coming decades.

Summary of the 10 Commitments to Action in the Rome Declaration on Nutrition

1. Eradicate hunger and prevent all forms of malnutrition worldwide

2. Increase investments for effective interventions and actions to improve people's diets and nutrition

3. Enhance sustainable food systems by developing coherent public policies from production to consumption and across relevant sectors

4. Raise the profile of nutrition within relevant national strategies, policies, action plans and programmes and align national resources accordingly

5. Improve nutrition by strengthening human and institutional capacities through relevant research and development, innovation and appropriate technology transfer

6. Strengthen and facilitate contributions and action by all stakeholders and promote collaboration within and across countries

7. Develop policies, programmes and initiatives for ensuring healthy diets throughout the life course

8. Empower people and create an enabling environment for making informed choices about food products for healthy dietary practices and appropriate infant and young child feeding practices through improved health and nutrition information and education

9. Implement the commitments of the Rome Declaration on Nutrition through the Framework for Action

10. Give due consideration to integrating the vision and commitments of the Rome Declaration on Nutrition into the post-2015 development agenda process including a possible related global goal

---

The Framework for Action (FFA) provides a set of voluntary policy options and strategies – in the form of 60 recommended actions – for use primarily by governments as well as other stakeholders, as appropriate, to guide the implementation of the political declaration.

This Information Note, prepared by the joint FAO and WHO Secretariat, is intended to accompany the FFA, and provides additional information that may be helpful to Member States and other stakeholders. For ease of reference, the document follows the structure of the FFA.

1.1 Background

There has been significant progress in reducing hunger and undernutrition since the 1992 International Conference on Nutrition (ICN), but progress has been uneven and unacceptably slow. The prevalence of those suffering from chronic dietary energy insufficiency has declined, but remains unacceptably high, with over 800 million people suffering from chronic undernourishment, mainly in South Asia and Sub-Saharan Africa.

Chronic malnutrition (stunting) still affects 161 million children under 5 years of age, while acute malnutrition (wasting) affects 51 million children under 5 years of age. In addition, over two billion people suffer from one or more micronutrient deficiencies.

Furthermore, alongside the problems of chronic undernourishment (hunger), undernutrition and micronutrient deficiencies (also referred to as 'hidden hunger'), most countries in the world are also facing increasing problems associated with obesity and diet-related noncommunicable diseases (NCDs). Over half a billion adults are obese and 42 million children under 5 years of age are overweight while diet-related NCDs are becoming serious global public health problems even in low- and middle-income countries, creating the "multiple burden" of malnutrition (hunger/undernutrition; micronutrient deficiencies; obesity and diet-related NCDs).

Meanwhile, the food system has continued to evolve with a greater proportion of food now processed and traded internationally. The availability of highly-processed commercial food products high in fat, sugars and salt/sodium has increased, often replacing healthy local diets and foods with the needed micronutrients, and resulting in excessive consumption of energy, fats, sugars and salt. The fundamental challenge today is to sustainably improve nutrition through implementation of coherent policies and better coordinated actions across all relevant sectors, strengthening, preserving and recovering healthy and sustainable food systems.

1.2 Purpose and Targets

The nature of this Framework for Action is voluntary. The purpose of the FFA is to guide implementation of the commitments of the Rome Declaration on Nutrition adopted by the Second International Conference on Nutrition held in Rome, Italy, on 19–21 November 2014. Building on existing commitments, goals and targets, the FFA provides a set of policy options and strategies which governments (including the European Union and other regional organizations on matters of their competency), acting in cooperation with other stakeholders, may incorporate, as appropriate, into their national nutrition, health, agriculture,[1] education, development and investment plans, and consider in negotiating international agreements to achieve better nutrition for all.

As governments have primary responsibility for taking action at country level, in dialogue with a wide range of stakeholders, including affected communities, the recommendations are principally addressed to government leaders. They will consider the appropriateness of the recommended policies and actions in relation to national and local needs and conditions, as well as national and regional priorities, including in legal frameworks. For the purpose of accountability, this FFA also adopts existing global targets for improving maternal, infant and young child nutrition[2] and for NCD risk factor reduction[3] to be achieved by 2025.

2. CREATING AN ENABLING ENVIRONMENT FOR EFFECTIVE ACTION

Following the 1992 ICN, many countries developed and implemented national nutrition strategies and action plans, reflecting their own priorities and strategies for alleviating hunger and malnutrition in all its forms. However, implementation and progress have been patchy and often unsatisfactory due to inadequate commitment and leadership, lack of financial investments, weak human and institutional capacities and lack of appropriate accountability mechanisms.

Actions to address malnutrition in all its forms are among the most cost-effective for development, providing very high economic returns. The potential human, societal and economic gains from turning the commitments of the Rome Declaration on Nutrition into action are substantial, while the costs of inaction are high. Available resources should be used to implement and scale up the most appropriate, cost-effective, evidence-based, nutrition interventions. This often requires complementary investments in other related sectors including food and agriculture, health, education, water, sanitation and hygiene, as well as trade.

Fulfilling the human right to food and fighting malnutrition in all its forms requires a sustained enabling policy environment and improved

---

[1] The term "agriculture" includes crops, livestock, forestry and fisheries.

[2] (1) 40% reduction of the global number of children under five who are stunted; (2) 50% reduction of anaemia in women of reproductive age; (3) 30% reduction of low birth weight; (4) no increase in childhood overweight; (5) increase exclusive breastfeeding rates in the first six months to at least 50%; (6) reduce and maintain childhood wasting to less than 5%.

[3] (1) Reduce salt intake by 30%; and (2) halt the increase in obesity prevalence in adolescents and adults.

governance mechanisms for food, health and related systems. Key requirements for the establishment of such enabling environment and improved governance mechanisms are:

- political commitment and leadership to prioritize structural, sustainable and equitable nutrition-enhancing approaches and strong national nutrition governance;

- adoption of effective and coherent policies, strategies and programmes, and effective multisectoral cooperation mechanisms, to address the structural determinants and causes of malnutrition, and its effects;

- increased and better aligned public and private investments in support of established nutrition goals;

- enhanced and sustained human and institutional capacities for effective action, including policy and programme design, management, monitoring and evaluation of nutrition outcomes and investments;

- allocation of national and international resources to ensure healthy diets for all, with special focus on the most nutritionally vulnerable life stages and specific dietary needs;

- engagement of trusted and trusting partners ready to align interests, and to create and sustain inclusive interaction;

- regular and systematic public assessments of progress to enhance accountability and effectiveness, and to improve resource use;

- international support for the implementation of national nutrition policies and programmes, as appropriate, and nutrition-sensitive approaches agreed at international level.

ICN2: Framework for Action

Taking the key required elements listed above into account, the FFA sets out a series of seven recommended actions to create an enabling environment and governance mechanisms for effective action (Recommendations 1–7):

- Recommendation 1: Enhance political commitment and social participation for improving nutrition at the country level through political dialogue and advocacy.

- Recommendation 2: Develop – or revise, as appropriate – and cost National Nutrition Plans, align policies that impact nutrition across different ministries and agencies, and strengthen legal frameworks and strategic capacities for nutrition.

- Recommendation 3: Strengthen and establish, as appropriate, national cross-government, inter-sector, multi-stakeholder mechanisms for food security and nutrition to oversee implementation of policies, strategies, programmes and other investments in nutrition. Such platforms may be needed at various levels, with robust safeguards against abuse and conflicts of interest.

- Recommendation 4: Increase responsible and sustainable investment in nutrition, especially at country level with domestic finance; generate additional resources through innovative financing tools; engage development partners to increase Official Development Assistance in nutrition and foster private investments as appropriate.

- Recommendation 5: Improve the availability, quality, quantity, coverage and management of multisectoral information systems related to food and nutrition for improved policy development and accountability.

- Recommendation 6: Promote inter-country collaboration, such as North–South, South–South and triangular cooperation, and information exchange on nutrition, food, technology, research, policies and programmes.

- Recommendation 7: Strengthen nutrition governance and coordinate policies, strategies and programmes of United Nations system agencies, programmes and funds within their respective mandates.

---

3. POLICY AND PROGRAMME OPTIONS TO IMPROVE NUTRITION IN ALL SECTORS

Addressing malnutrition in all its forms is strengthened by a common vision and a multisectoral approach that includes coordinated, coherent, equitable and complementary interventions[4] in food systems and agriculture,[5] health, social protection, education and trade among others, and by addressing not only hunger and undernutrition, but also the multiple burden of malnutrition efficiently and innovatively.

3.1 Sustainable Food Systems Promoting Healthy Diets[6]

The types of foods produced and how they are processed, traded, retailed and marketed through the supply chain impact the collective surroundings, opportunities and conditions that influence people's food and beverage choices and dietary practices and consequently, their nutritional status. Information and education concerning dietary practices are vital, but consumers must also be empowered through enabling food environments.[7] Food environments that provide safe, diverse and healthy diets are particularly important for vulnerable groups, who are more constrained by lack of resources.

A food system approach – from production to processing, storage, transportation, marketing, retailing and consumption – is thus key to promote healthy diet and improve nutrition as isolated interventions have limited impact.

Since food systems have become increasingly complex and strongly influence people's ability to consume healthy diets, coherent action and innovative food system solutions are needed tability to consume healthy diets, coherent action and innovative food system solutions are needed to ensure access to sustainable, balanced and healthy diets for all. These solutions should include production, availability, accessibility and affordability of a variety of cereals, legumes, vegetables, fruits and animal source foods,

---

[4] The term "interventions" refers to those actions (policies and programmes) designed to address immediate and/or underlying determinants of nutrition among individuals and households.

[5] As defined in the ICN2 Declaration, the term agriculture comprises crops, livestock, forestry and fisheries.

[6] A healthy diet refers to a balanced, diverse and appropriate selection of foods eaten over a period of time. A healthy diet ensures that the needs for essential macronutrients (proteins, fats and carbohydrates including dietary fibres) and micronutrients (vitamins, minerals and trace elements) are met specific to the person's gender, age, physical activity level and physiological state. WHO indicates that for diets to be healthy (a) daily needs of energy, vitamins and minerals should be met, but energy intake should not exceed needs; (b) consumption of fruit and vegetables is over 400 g per day; (c) intake of saturated fats is less than 10% of total energy intake; (d) intake of trans-fats is less than 1% of total energy intake; (e) intake of free sugars is less than 10% of total energy intake or, preferably, less than 5%; (f) intake of salt is less than 5 g per day. For more information, see the WHO Fact Sheet on Healthy Diet (Fact sheet No 394, September 2014, http://www.who.int/mediacentre/factsheets/fs394/en/).

[7] Food environments are the collective surroundings, opportunities and conditions that influence people's food and beverage choices and nutritional status.

including fish, meat, eggs and dairy products; diets containing adequate macronutrients (carbohydrates, fats and protein), fibre and essential micronutrients (vitamins and minerals) in line with WHO recommendations on healthy diet, and produced and consumed sustainably. On the other hand, these solutions should include measures to restrict the production, availability, accessibility and promotion of food products leading to excessive intake of energy, fats, sugars and salt/sodium.

Globally, the food system contains a diverse mix of traditional and modern supply chains. Both offer risks and opportunities for nutrition. Low-income consumers in low and middle income countries have a greater tendency to buy food via traditional supply chains, where losses are high, and safety and quality control are limited. Modern processing and retailing offer more fruits, vegetables and animal-source foods through cold chain storage, and contribute to improved food quality and safety, but highly processed foods of low nutritional value contribute to rising obesity and diet-related NCDs.

Investing in rural populations is vital for equitable human development. Subsistence and family farmers, most of whom are women, and often lack access to and control of critical inputs and markets, can be more effectively engaged to meet local nutrition needs, while commercial producers are critical to stabilizing global supply and prices, and to applying sustainable practices at scale.

Raising women's incomes brings great health and nutrition benefits as often women manage household resources and greatly influence household food consumption, in particular of infants and young children. Improving agriculture and food technology gives women more time, improves their incomes and nutrition, and generally enhances their well-being as well as their infants and young children. It is also important to increase women's control over resources such as income, land, agricultural inputs and technology.

Natural and manmade disasters, emergencies, conflicts and shocks have increased in recent years, in both frequency and intensity. Resilience is necessary to prevent further deterioration of the nutritional status of crisis-affected populations, while nutrition is critical to strengthening both community and individual resilience. Resilience requires that preventive and curative interventions to address the underlying causes of malnutrition are implemented before, during and after crises.

Climate change affects production and productivity, and this directly affects diets and nutrition, smallholder farmer[8] incomes, as well as food price volatility. Food systems themselves have a major impact on the

---

[8] Smallholder farmers here also refer to agriculture and food workers, artisanal fisherfolk, pastoralists, indigenous peoples and the landless. See Committee on World Food Security, Global Strategic Framework for Food Security and Nutrition, 2013.

environment.[9] Some food production systems have the potential to reduce emissions intensity significantly. Food loss and waste should be reduced to

---

ICN2: Framework for Action

The Framework for Action lists the following nine recommended actions for sustainable food systems promoting healthy diets (Recommendations 8–16):

- Recommendation 8: Review national policies and investments and integrate nutrition objectives into food and agriculture policy, programme design and implementation, to enhance nutrition sensitive agriculture, ensure food security and enable healthy diets.

- Recommendation 9: Strengthen local food production and processing, especially by smallholder and family farmers, giving special attention to women's empowerment, while recognizing that efficient and effective trade is key to achieving nutrition objectives.

- Recommendation 10: Promote the diversification of crops including underutilized traditional crops, more production of fruits and vegetables, and appropriate production of animal-source products as needed, applying sustainable food production and natural resource management practices.

- Recommendation 11: Improve storage, preservation, transport and distribution technologies and infrastructure to reduce seasonal food insecurity, food and nutrient loss and waste.

- Recommendation 12: Establish and strengthen institutions, policies, programmes and services to enhance the resilience of the food supply in crisis-prone areas, including areas affected by climate change.

- Recommendation 13: Develop, adopt and adapt, where appropriate, international guidelines on healthy diets.

- Recommendation 14: Encourage gradual reduction of saturated fat, sugars and salt/sodium and trans-fat from foods and beverages to prevent excessive intake by consumers and improve nutrient content of foods, as needed.

- Recommendation 15: Explore regulatory and voluntary instruments – such as marketing, publicity and labelling policies, economic incentives or disincentives in accordance with Codex Alimentarius and World Trade Organization rules – to promote healthy diets.

- Recommendation 16: Establish food or nutrient-based standards to make healthy diets and safe drinking water accessible in public facilities such as hospitals, childcare facilities, workplaces, universities, schools, food and catering services, government offices and prisons, and encourage the establishment of facilities for breastfeeding.

---

[9] The two major contributions of agriculture to the atmospheric composition and climate are due to deforestation and animal husbandry – of which food production and consumption constitute a significant share. The potential for biological carbon sequestration is compromised by tillage. See FAOSTAT, Greenhouse Gas Emissions from Agriculture, April 2014.

improve food system efficacy and sustainability. There is an urgent need, therefore, to develop more sustainable food systems by encouraging sustainable food production and consumption practices. Agreement on shared principles of sustainability in promoting healthy diets is needed, and this will require policy coherence among the environment, agriculture and food sectors.

3.2 International Trade and Investment

Trade and investment have become increasingly important to food systems. Trade and investment agreements affect how the food system functions at global, regional, national and local levels, influencing food prices, availability, access and consumption as well as nutrition outcomes, food safety and dietary options.

Coherence between trade and nutrition policy is vital. Trade policy should support and provide adequate flexibility to implement effective nutrition policies and programmes. While trade has substantially increased the availability of and sometimes access to food for people, trade policies and agreements should not negatively impact the human right to food. Implementation of the World Trade Organization Agreement on Trade-Related Aspects of Intellectual Property Rights should be supportive of food security and nutrition, and the obligation of Member States to promote, realize and protect the human right to food. The recommendations of Codex Alimentarius are also key for ensuring that international trade respects and promotes health and nutrition.

ICN2: Framework for Action

The FFA sets out the following two recommended actions for international trade and investment (Recommendations 17–18):

- Recommendation 17: Encourage governments, United Nations agencies, programmes and funds, the World Trade Organization and other international organizations to identify opportunities to achieve global food and nutrition targets, through trade and investment policies.

- Recommendation 18: Improve the availability and access of the food supply through appropriate trade agreements and policies and endeavour to ensure that such agreements and policies do not have a negative impact on the right to adequate food in other countries.[10]

---

[10] United Nations General Assembly resolution A/RES/68/177, paragraph 25.

3.3 Nutrition Education[11] and Information

Knowledge and education empower people to make informed healthy dietary and lifestyle choices, to improve infant and young child feeding practices and care, and to improve hygiene and health promoting behaviour. Lifestyle and behaviour change is an important objective of nutrition education. It can also help reduce food losses and waste and boost sustainable resource use.

Governments, nongovernmental organizations (NGOs), the private sector and nutrition advocates should lead by example and can help promote desired healthy lifestyle changes, including through active and accessible quality health and agricultural inputs and services, food and nutrition knowledge and skills included in primary and secondary school curricula (including teaching hygiene, food preparation and culinary practices in schools), public nutrition information, social marketing campaigns, and regulations on nutrient and health claims.

Health services should be more active in nutrition education; dietary counselling should be part of primary health care, and nutrition counselling part of health workers' training. Pre-natal and post-natal dietary counselling can significantly improve maternal and child nutrition. Adolescent girls and women in particular will benefit from better nutrition education to promote exclusive breastfeeding in the first six months of life and appropriate infant and young child feeding. Educational outreach should extend to husbands, fathers and other caregivers.

People should be informed of the nutritional content of food and meals at the time of purchase through easy-to-understand nutrition labels. Regulations on nutrient and health claims are also needed to safeguard consumers.

---

[11] The term 'nutrition education' refers to education and information dissemination efforts including promotion, advocacy, information, communication, counselling, empowerment, consumer education, behavioral change communication and 'social marketing at individual, community, national and international levels to promote voluntary adoption of food choices and other food- and nutrition-related behaviours conducive to health and well-being.

ICN2: Framework for Action

The FFA sets out the following three recommended actions for nutrition education and information (Recommendations 19–21):

- Recommendation 19: Implement nutrition education and information interventions based on national dietary guidelines and coherent policies related to food and diets, through improved school curricula, nutrition education in the health, agriculture and social protection services, community interventions and point-of-sale information, including labelling.

- Recommendation 20: Build nutrition skills and capacity to undertake nutrition education activities, particularly for front line workers, social workers, agricultural extension personnel, teachers and health professionals.

- Recommendation 21: Conduct appropriate social marketing campaigns and lifestyle change communication programmes to promote physical activity, dietary diversification, consumption of micronutrient-rich foods such as fruits and vegetables, including traditional local foods and taking into consideration cultural aspects, better child and maternal nutrition, appropriate care practices and adequate breastfeeding and complementary feeding, targeted and adapted for different audiences and stakeholders in the food system.

3.4 Social Protection

In 2012, the UN General Assembly recommended comprehensive universal social protection beginning with basic or minimum 'social protection floors'. Given the limited and uneven progress in reducing poverty, hunger, food insecurity and malnutrition, and the currently dim prospects for economic and employment growth in much of the world, comprehensive social protection is needed to eliminate poverty and malnutrition in all its forms.

Social protection measures, such as food distribution, cash transfers, decent job creation and school feeding, can increase incomes and strengthen resilience. When combined with relevant health services, well-designed social protection programmes result in improved height, reduced anaemia, increased dietary diversity, and raised consumption of nutrient-dense foods, especially in low-income households with infants and children.

These measures can substantially enhance small producer resilience by preventing destitution in times of crisis besides raising production and productivity, both on- and off-farm, taking into account local contexts and market capabilities.

ICN2: Framework for Action

The FFA sets out the following three recommended actions for social protection (Recommendations 22–24):

- Recommendation 22: Incorporate nutrition objectives into social protection programmes and into humanitarian assistance safety net programmes.

- Recommendation 23: Use cash and food transfers, including school feeding programmes and other forms of social protection for vulnerable populations to improve diets through better access to food which conforms with the beliefs, culture, traditions, dietary habits and preferences of individuals in accordance with national and international laws and obligations, and which is nutritionally adequate for healthy diets.

- Recommendation 24: Increase income for the most vulnerable populations by creating decent jobs for all, including through the promotion of self-employment.

3.5 Strong and Resilient Health Systems

Health systems are increasingly challenged to tackle the evolving needs presented by the multiple forms of malnutrition and their health consequences. Strong health systems are needed to prevent and treat malnutrition in all its forms through the delivery of evidence-informed nutrition interventions, as well as to prevent and treat recurrent infections which can aggravate undernutrition. In addition, health systems also have to deal with the long-term health consequences associated with overweight and obesity, and the prevention and control of diet-related NCDs.

Effective delivery of direct nutrition interventions as well as prevention and treatment of diseases which can aggravate nutrition problems require strong and resilient national health systems. Health systems need to be linked to and coherent with food systems, and both need to strive for equity and the full realization of the right to enjoy the highest attainable standard of physical and mental health and the right to food.

Access to health services and financial risk protection for all – including the most marginalized and most vulnerable – is needed. This means universal health coverage (UHC), which implies that all people have access, without discrimination, to nationally determined sets of the needed promotive, preventive, curative, palliative and rehabilitative essential health services and essential, safe, affordable, effective and quality medicines, while ensuring that the use of these services does not expose the users to financial hardship with a special emphasis on the poor, vulnerable and marginalized segments of the population.[12] Achieving UHC will lead to stronger, more efficient and more equitable health systems.

ICN2: Framework for Action

The FFA sets out the following four recommended actions for strong and resilient health systems (Recommendations 25–28):

- Recommendation 25: Strengthen health systems and promote universal health coverage[13], particularly through primary health care, to enable national health systems to address malnutrition in all its forms.

- Recommendation 26: Improve the integration of nutrition actions into health systems through appropriate strategies for strengthening human resources, leadership and governance, health system financing and service delivery, as well as the provision of essential medicines, information and monitoring.

- Recommendation 27: Promote universal access to all direct nutrition actions and relevant health actions impacting nutrition through health programmes.

- Recommendation 28: Implement the WHO Global Strategy on Infant and Young Child Feeding, the WHO Comprehensive Implementation Plan on Maternal, Infant and Young Child Nutrition 2012–2025, and the WHO Global Action Plan for the Prevention and Control of Noncommunicable Diseases 2013–2020 through commensurate financing and adequate policies.

3.5.1 Delivery of direct nutrition interventions

In developing policies and programmes to address nutrition challenges, it is imperative to give special attention to the nutrition of mothers, infants and young children. Although different age-groups need appropriate attention, as identified in the life course approach (e.g. pre-school children, adolescent girls), ensuring appropriate nutrition during the first 1,000 days is especially critical, and has a lasting impact on the survival, health and development of the individual.

Due to contemporary demographic transitions and resulting changes in the age structures of populations – with increased proportions of the elderly

---

[12] World Health Assembly Resolution A67.14. Available at: apps.who.int/gb/ebwha/pdf_-files/WHA67/A67_R14-en.pdf

[13] In accordance with preambular paragraph 9 of resolution WHA67.14, universal health coverage implies that all people have access, without discrimination, to nationally determined sets of needed promotive, preventive, curative, palliative and rehabilitative essential health services and essential, safe, affordable, effective and quality medicines, while ensuring that the use of these services does not expose users, especially the poor, vulnerable and marginalized segments of the population, to financial hardship.

– actions are also required to provide adequate health and nutrition support to address the specific needs of the elderly. Direct nutrition interventions need to be integrated and implemented together with nutrition-sensitive interventions.

Promote, protect and support breastfeeding

Breastfeeding is one of the most effective ways to improve child survival and to promote healthy child growth and development. It needs to be promoted, protected and supported in all circumstances. Exclusive breastfeeding[14] in the first six months of life ensures adequate, affordable, acceptable, appropriate and readily available food security and nutrition on a continuing basis. Breastfeeding contributes to enjoyment of the highest attainable

---

ICN2: Framework for Action

The FFA sets out the following five recommended actions to promote, protect and support breastfeeding (Recommendations 29–33):

- Recommendation 29: Adapt and implement the International Code of Marketing of Breast-milk Substitutes and subsequent relevant World Health Assembly resolutions.

- Recommendation 30: Implement policies and practices, including labour reforms, as appropriate, to promote protection of working mothers.[15]

- Recommendation 31: Implement policies, programmes and actions to ensure that health services promote, protect and support breastfeeding, including the Baby-Friendly Hospital Initiative.

- Recommendation 32: Encourage and promote – through advocacy, education and capacity building – an enabling environment where men, particularly fathers, participate actively and share responsibilities with mothers in caring for their infants and young children, while empowering women and enhancing their health and nutritional status throughout the life course.

- Recommendation 33: Ensure that policies and practices in emergency situations and humanitarian crises promote, protect and support breastfeeding.

---

[14] WHO recommends early initiation of breastfeeding (in the first hour), and exclusive breastfeeding for the first six months of life to achieve optimal growth, development and health, followed by nutritionally adequate and safe complementary feeding while breastfeeding continues for up to two years of age or beyond.

[15] As specified in the International Labour Organization's Maternity Protection Convention No. 183 and the corresponding Recommendation 191.

standard of health as recognized in the Convention on the Rights of the Child. The International Code of marketing Breast-milk substitutes needs to be adopted through the legislative tools that each country has, to protect breastfeeding. The FFA adopts the global target to increase the rate of exclusive breastfeeding in the first six months up to at least 50% by 2025.

Wasting

Severely wasted children are estimated to be, on average, 11 times more likely to die than their healthy counterparts.[16] The global target to reduce and maintain childhood wasting to less than 5% by 2025 is adopted by the FFA. Both moderate and severe wasting can be addressed by the community-based management of malnutrition approach, comprising of treatment and community awareness raising to facilitate early detection and treatment. Globally, only around 14% of wasted children are currently being reached by treatment services.

ICN2: Framework for Action

The FFA sets out the following two recommendations to address wasting (Recommendations 34–35):

- Recommendation 34: Adopt policies and actions, and mobilize funding, to improve coverage of treatment for wasting, using the community-based management of acute malnutrition approach and improve the integrated management of childhood illnesses.

- Recommendation 35: Integrate disaster and emergency preparedness into relevant policies and programmes.

Stunting

Childhood stunting remains one of the world's most fundamental challenges for improved human development. The global target of 40% reduction in the number of stunted children under five years of age is adopted by the FFA. Stunting results from a complex web of individual, household, environmental, socioeconomic, political and cultural influences. Direct nutrition interventions need to be integrated and implemented together with nutrition-sensitive interventions and actions on social protection, health system strengthening, breastfeeding, prevention and treatment of diarrhoea and other infectious diseases, water, sanitation and hygiene, reproductive health and food safety.

---

[16] WHO. Global Nutrition Targets 2025: Reduce and maintain childhood wasting to less than 5%. WHO Policy Brief, Geneva, 2014.

Actions to prevent wasting have direct impacts on stunting, e.g. by enabling the early detection and treatment of stunting. Therefore, actions to address wasting and stunting should be coordinated and integrated for better results.

ICN2: Framework for Action

The FFA sets out the following two recommendations to address stunting (Recommendations 36–37):

- Recommendation 36: Establish policies and strengthen interventions to improve maternal nutrition and health, beginning with adolescent girls and continuing through pregnancy and lactation.

- Recommendation 37: Establish health policies, programmes and strategies to promote optimal infant and young child feeding, particularly exclusive breastfeeding up to six months, followed by adequate complementary feeding (from six to 24 months).

Childhood overweight and obesity

Overweight and obese children are at higher risk of developing serious health problems, including type 2 diabetes, high blood pressure, asthma, other respiratory problems, sleep disorders and liver diseases. They may also suffer from psychological effects, such as low self-esteem, depression and social isolation. Childhood overweight and obesity also increase the risk of adult obesity, NCDs, premature death and disability in adulthood. Actions to prevent and address childhood overweight and obesity should start with breastfeeding promotion (considering its role in reducing the risk of childhood obesity), healthy school feeding programmes (with the provision of fresh fruits and vegetables at schools as well as the restriction of sugar-sweetened beverage consumption) and other policies and programmes that address the social determinants of health. Food marketing powerfully influences people's food choices. Excessive marketing pressure, particularly on children, has promoted unhealthy dietary practices. Measures to limit such influences are therefore needed. Stronger actions at the global level are required for reducing and preventing childhood overweight and obesity – in line with the global target of no increase in childhood overweight by 2025 – alongside actions to address undernutrition problems.

ICN2: Framework for Action

The FFA sets out the following four recommendations to address childhood overweight and obesity (Recommendations 38–41):

- Recommendation 38: Provide dietary counselling to women during pregnancy for healthy weight gain and adequate nutrition.
- Recommendation 39: Improve child nutritional status and growth, particularly by addressing maternal exposure to the availability and marketing of complementary foods, and by improving supplementary feeding programmes for infants and young children.
- Recommendation 40: Regulate the marketing of food and non-alcoholic beverages to children in accordance with WHO recommendations.
- Recommendation 41: Create a conducive environment that promotes physical activity to address sedentary lifestyle from the early stages of life.

Anaemia in women of reproductive age

Lack of vitamins and minerals presents a global public health problem. Iodine, vitamin A and iron deficiencies are the most important globally, and present a major threat to health and development. Iron deficiency anaemia, the most common and widespread nutritional disorder in the world, especially impairs the health and wellbeing of women. Anaemia increases the risk of maternal and neonatal adversities. Failure to improve anaemia consigns millions of women to impaired health and quality of life, generations of children to impaired development and learning, and communities and nations to reduced economic productivity. In order to achieve the global target of a 50% reduction in anaemia in women of reproductive age by 2025, direct nutrition interventions need to be implemented together with strategies to promote healthy and diversified diets are needed. Implementation of recommendations on provision of healthy diets in schools and preschools, provision of nutrition education, treatment and prevention of infectious disease and improved hygiene and sanitation is also important.

ICN2: Framework for Action

The FFA sets out the following two recommended actions to address anaemia in women of reproductive age (Recommendations 42–43):

- Recommendation 42: Improve intake of micronutrients through consumption of nutrient-dense foods, especially foods rich in iron, where necessary, through fortification and supplementation strategies, and promote healthy and diversified diets.

- Recommendation 43: Provide daily iron and folic acid and other micronutrient supplementation to pregnant women as part of antenatal care; and intermittent iron and folic acid supplementation to menstruating women where the prevalence of anaemia is 20% or higher, and deworming, where appropriate.

3.5.2 Interventions in health services to improve nutrition

Besides delivering interventions that directly improve nutrition, health systems also need to deliver other interventions that impact on nutrition, including promoting health, preventing and treating infections, and improving women's reproductive health.

Frequent bouts of infectious diseases, such as acute enteric infections, are an important cause of child undernutrition, helping to explain why child undernutrition still exists in populations which are generally food secure. Infectious diseases – such as malaria, HIV/AIDS, tuberculosis and some neglected tropical diseases – contribute to the high prevalence of iron deficiency anaemia and undernutrition in some areas. Worm infestations can impair nutritional status by causing internal bleeding, diarrhoea and poor absorption of nutrients. Infections can also cause a loss of appetite which, in turn, can lead to reduced nutrient intake. Breastfeeding is one way to provide protection for infants against infections in circumstances of poor sanitation.

Access to integral health care services that ensure adequate support for safe pregnancy and delivery for all women is critical to be able to improve maternal and child health, and to break the intergenerational cycle of malnutrition in all its forms. Adolescent pregnancy is associated with higher risk of maternal mortality and morbidity, stillbirths, neonatal deaths, preterm births and low birth weight. Women who have very closely spaced pregnancies are more likely to have maternal anaemia and preterm or low-birth-weight babies. Efforts to prevent adolescent pregnancy and to encourage pregnancy spacing are therefore needed.

ICN2: Framework for Action

The FFA includes the following six recommendations on health services to improve nutrition (Recommendations 44–49):

- Recommendation 44: Implement policies and programmes to ensure universal access to and use of insecticide-treated nets, and to provide preventive malaria treatment for pregnant women in areas with moderate to high malaria transmission.

- Recommendation 45: Provide periodic deworming for all school-age children in endemic areas.

- Recommendation 46: Implement policies and programmes to improve health service capacity to prevent and treat infectious diseases.[17]

- Recommendation 47: Provide zinc supplementation to reduce the duration and severity of diarrhoea, and to prevent subsequent episodes in children.

- Recommendation 48: Provide iron and, among others, vitamin A supplementation for pre-school children to reduce the risk of anaemia.

- Recommendation 49: Implement policies and strategies to ensure that women have comprehensive information and access to integral health care services that ensure adequate support for safe pregnancy and delivery.

3.6 Water, Sanitation, and Hygiene

Water is a finite resource essential throughout the food system – from production to consumption. Agriculture and food production accounts for more than two thirds of freshwater withdrawals.[18] To achieve sustainable, healthy diets, more rational water use will be required, along with changes to consumption patterns. To meet this challenge, food production systems need to adapt with a combination of relevant measures. Greater water use conservation, along with other relevant measures to reduce food – including water – waste and loss, are required to achieve sustainability.

Access to safe drinking water and adequate sanitation is recognized as a human right[19] essential for health, prevention of diarrhoeal disease, and thus

---

[17] Including prevention of mother-to-child transmission of HIV, immunization against measles, and antibiotic treatment for girls with urinary infections.

[18] Water in a changing world. United Nations World Water Development Report 3. World Water Assessment Programme. UNESCO/Earthscan, 2009.

[19] The main international treaties explicitly recognizing the right to water include the 1979 Convention on the Elimination of All Forms of Discrimination Against Women (CEDAW, Art.14{[}2{]}) and the 1989 Convention on the Rights of the Child (CRC, Art. 24). The main political declarations were passed by the UN General Assembly and the UN Human Rights Council, both in 2010.

to improve nutrition. Diarrhoea is the second leading cause of death among children under five, and lack of safe drinking water – along with inadequate sanitation and hygiene – are major risk factors. Children who are affected by undernutrition are more likely to die from diarrhoea. In turn, diarrhoea undermines nutrition by reducing appetite and food absorption.

Over one billion people still practice open defecation. In line with the global call to action on sanitation, efforts should focus on improving hygiene, changing social norms, better management of human waste and waste-water, and completely eliminating the practice of open defecation by 2025.

ICN2: Framework for Action

The FFA sets out the following three recommended actions on water, sanitation and hygiene (Recommendations 50–52):

- Recommendation 50: Implement policies and programmes using participatory approaches to improve water management in agriculture and food production.[20]

- Recommendation 51: Invest in and commit to achieve universal access to safe drinking water, with the participation of civil society and the support of international partners, as appropriate.

- Recommendation 52: Implement policies and strategies using participatory approaches to ensure universal access to adequate sanitation[21] and to promote safe hygiene practices, including hand washing with soap.

3.7 Food Safety and Antimicrobial Resistance (AMR)

Food safety needs to be integrated into the global food security and nutrition agenda to make significant progress in improving nutrition. Food safety problems threaten the nutritional status of populations, particularly vulnerable groups like the elderly, pregnant women and children. Food contaminated by chemical or biological hazards, including environmental pollutants, is the origin of many diseases, ranging from diarrhoea to cancer, undermining people's lives, health and nutrition well- being, directly and indirectly.[22]

---

[20] Including by reducing water wastage in irrigation, strategies for multiple use of water (including wastewater), and better use of appropriate technology.

[21] Including by implementing effective risk assessment and management practices on safe wastewater use and sanitation.

[22] WHO Initiative to Estimate the Global Burden of Foodborne Disease. http://www.who.int/foodsafety/foodborne_disease/FERG2_report.pdf

Morbidity due to diarrhoea, dysentery and other enteric diseases – arising from unsafe food, contaminated water and poor sanitation – has not declined much over recent decades. In some developing countries, children are chronically exposed, through their diets, to aflatoxins, which are not only carcinogenic, but also probably contribute to stunting.

ICN2: Framework for Action

The FFA sets out the following five recommended actions on food safety and antimicrobial resistance (AMR) (Recommendations 53–57):

- Recommendation 53: Develop, establish, enforce and strengthen, as appropriate, food control systems, including reviewing and modernizing national food safety legislation and regulations to ensure that food producers and suppliers throughout the food chain operate responsibly.

- Recommendation 54: Actively take part in the work of the Codex Alimentarius Commission on nutrition and food safety, and implement, as appropriate, internationally adopted standards at the national level.

- Recommendation 55: Participate in and contribute to international networks to exchange food safety information, including for managing emergencies.[23]

- Recommendation 56: Raise awareness among relevant stakeholders on the problems posed by antimicrobial resistance, and implement appropriate multisectoral measures to address antimicrobial resistance, including prudent use of antimicrobials in veterinary and human medicine.

- Recommendation 57: Develop and implement national guidelines on prudent use of antimicrobials in food-producing animals[24] according to internationally recognized standards adopted by competent international organizations to reduce non-therapeutic use of antimicrobials and to phase out the use of antimicrobials as growth promoters in the absence of risk analysis as described in Codex Code of Practice CAC/RCP61-2005.

One emerging food safety issue of global concern is antimicrobial resistance (AMR). While antimicrobial drugs are essential for both human and animal health and welfare, and critical to food producers' livelihoods, their misuse has led to growing AMR threats to humans and agro–ecological

---

[23] FAO/WHO International Network of Food Safety Authorities (http://www.who.int/foodsafety/areas_work/infosan/en/).

[24] The term refers to animals used for the purpose of food production. Monitoring frameworks may be developed based on the Global Monitoring Framework for Maternal, Infant and Young Child Nutrition, the Monitoring Framework for the Global Action Plan on Noncommunicable Diseases, as well as on the monitoring of food security including indicators of FAO prevalence of undernourishment, food insecurity experience scale, and other widely used indicators.

environments. Addressing AMR therefore requires a multisectoral "One Health Approach", but significant challenges still remain in translating internationally recognized standards and guidelines into appropriate national policies and actions.[25]

4 FOLLOW-UP AFTER ICN2

Endorsement by the United Nations General Assembly (UNGA)

The United Nations system – and particularly FAO and WHO – has an important role to play in supporting national and regional efforts, enhancing international cooperation and monitoring follow-up to the ICN2.

The ICN2 Rome Declaration on Nutrition recommends the United Nations General Assembly to endorse the commitments as well as the policy options provided in the FFA for implementation. Endorsement by the UNGA ensures high-level political commitment to address nutrition challenges across sectors, and the involvement of a wide range of UN agencies, programmes and funds, as well as other international and regional organizations, in achieving the commitments of the Rome Declaration on Nutrition and supporting implementation of actions recommended in the FFA within their respective mandates. Engagement of the UNGA will also facilitate more direct input and links to the development and implementation of the Post-2015 Sustainable Development Goals.

Time Frame for Implementation of the FFA

The actions recommended by the FFA will be implemented over a ten-year time frame (2016–2025), in line with the Rome Declaration on Nutrition.

Accountability Mechanisms

Effective mechanisms for accountability are essential for ensuring that the commitments of the Rome Declaration on Nutrition are followed through, to track progress being made, and to enable people to hold duty bearers, policymakers and institutions accountable.

---

[25] There have been several initiatives led by FAO, WHO, the World Organization for Animal Health (OIE) and the Codex Alimentarius Commission. http://www.fao.org/ag/againfo/home/en/news_archive/2011_04_amr.html http://www.who.int/foodsafety/areas_work/antimicrobial-resistance/en/ http://www.oie.int/for-the-media/amr/ Code of Practice to Minimize and Contain Antimicrobial Resistance, CAC/RCP 61- 2005, http://www.codexalimentarius.org/download/standards/10213/CXP_061e.pdf; Guidelines for Risk Analysis of Foodborne Antimicrobial Resistance, CAC/GL 77-2011, http://www.codexalimentarius.org/download/standards/11776/CXG_077e.pdf

ICN2: Framework for Action

The FFA sets out the following three recommended actions to ensure accountability (Recommendations 58–60):

- Recommendation 58: National governments are encouraged to establish nutrition targets and intermediate milestones, consistent with the timeframe for implementation (2016–2025), as well as global nutrition and noncommunicable disease targets established by the World Health Assembly. They are invited to include – in their national monitoring frameworks – agreed international indicators for nutrition outcomes (to track progress in achieving national targets), nutrition programme implementation (including coverage of interventions) and the nutrition policy environment (including institutional arrangements, capacities and investments in nutrition). Monitoring should be conducted, to the fullest possible extent, through existing mechanisms.

- Recommendation 59: Reports on implementation of the commitments of the Rome Declaration on Nutrition will be compiled jointly by FAO and WHO, in close collaboration with other United Nations agencies, funds and programmes and other relevant regional and international organizations, as appropriate, based on country self-assessments as well as information available through other monitoring and accountability mechanisms (e.g. Scaling Up Nutrition self-assessment reports, reports to the FAO Conference and the World Health Assembly, and the Global Nutrition Report).

- Recommendation 60: The governing bodies of FAO and WHO, and other relevant international organizations are requested to consider the inclusion of reports on the overall follow-up to ICN2 on the agendas of the regular FAO and WHO governing body meetings, including FAO regional conferences and WHO regional committee meetings, possibly on a biennial basis. The Directors-General of FAO and WHO are also requested to transmit such reports to the United Nations General Assembly as appropriate.

Bibliography

Ahmed, Akhter U., Quisumbing, Agnes R., Nasreen, Mahbuba, Hoddinott, John F., and Bryan, Elizabeth (2009), *Comparing food and cash transfers to the ultra poor in Bangladesh*, International Food Policy Research Institute, Washington, DC.

Ajemian, Shoghag Sherry (2014), *Social protection and an enabling environment for the right to adequate food*, Right to Food Thematic Study 5, Food and Agriculture Organization of the United Nations, Rome, URL: www.fao.org/3/a-i3894e.pdf.

Alderman, Harold, and Behrman, Jere R. (2004), *Estimated economic benefits of reducing low birth weight in low-income countries*, World Bank HNP Discussion Paper, The World Bank, Washington, DC, URL: siteresources. worldbank . org / healthnutritionandpopulation / Resources / 281627 - 1095698140167/Alderman-ReduceLowBirthWeight_whole.pdf.

Alderman, Harold, Elder, Leslie, Goyal, Aparajita, Herforth, Anna, Hoberg, Yurie Tanimichi, Marini, Alessandra, Ruel-Bergeron, Julie, Saavedra, Jaime, Shekar, Meera, Tiwari, Sailesh, and Zaman, Hassan (2013), *Improving nutrition through multisectoral approaches*, The World Bank, Washington, DC.

Ali, Amjad, Khan, M.M., Malik, Z.U., Charania, Barkat Ali, Bhojani, Faiyaz A., and Baig, Shahid Mahmood (1992), "Impact of the long term supply of iodised salt to the endemic goitre area", *Journal of Pakistan Medical Association*, 42(6), pp. 138–40.

Ali, Mubarik, and Tsou, Samson C.S. (1997), "Combating micronutrient deficiencies through vegetables: A neglected food frontier in Asia", *Food Policy*, 22(1), pp. 17–38.

Allen, Lindsay H., De Benoist, Bruno, Dary, Omar, and Hurrell, Richard, eds. (2006), *Guidelines on food fortification with micronutrients*, World Health Organization, Geneva, and Food and Agricultural Organization, Rome.

Alloway, B.J. (2009), "Soil factors associated with zinc deficiency in crops and humans", *Environmental Geochemistry and Health*, 31(5), pp. 537–48.

Anand, Sudhir, and Kanbur, S.M. Ravi (1991), "Public policy and basic needs provision: intervention and achievement in Sri Lanka", in Drèze, Jean, and Sen, Amartya, eds., *The political economy of hunger, Volume 3: Endemic hunger*, WIDER Studies in Development Economics, Clarendon Press, Oxford.

Andrieu, Elise, Darmon, Nicole, and Drewnowski, Adam (2006), "Low-cost diets: More energy, fewer nutrients", *European Journal of Clinical Nutrition*, 60(3), pp. 434–36.

Aro, Antti, Alfthan, Georg, and Varo, Pertti (1995), "Effects of supplementation of fertilizers on human selenium status in Finland", *Analyst*, 120(3), pp. 841–43.

Asfaw, Solomon, Covarrubias, Katia, Daidone, Silvio, Davis, Benjamin, Dewbre, Josh, Djebbari, Habiba, Romeo, Alessandro, and Winters, Paul (2012), *Analytical framework for evaluating the productive impact of cash transfer programmes on household behaviour: Methodological guidelines for the From Protection to Production (PtoP) project*, Food and Agriculture Organization of the United Nations, Rome, URL: www.fao.org/docrep/018/aq663e/aq663e.pdf.

Barrett, Christopher B., and Maxwell, Daniel G. (2005), *Food aid after fifty years: Recasting its role*, Routledge, London and New York.

Baxter, Jo-Anna, and Zlotkin, Stanley (2015), "Compendium of evidence on double fortified salt", Solutions for Hidden Hunger, Micronutrient Initiative, URL: www.micronutrient.org/CMFiles/DFS-Compendium-DRAFT-2015-02-04.pdf.

Beinner, Mark Anthony, and Lamounier, Joel Alves (2003), "Recent experience with fortification of foods and beverages with iron for the control of iron-deficiency anemia in Brazilian children", *Food and Nutrition Bulletin*, 24(3), pp. 268–74.

Benson, Todd (2011), "Cross-sectoral coordination in the public sector: A challenge to leveraging agriculture for improving nutrition and health", Conference on Leveraging Agriculture for Improving Nutrition and Health, 2020, Conference Brief 10, New Delhi.

Berti, Peter R., Krasevec, Julia, and FitzGerald, Sian (2004), "A review of the effectiveness of agriculture interventions in improving nutrition outcomes", *Public Health Nutrition*, 7(5), pp. 599–609.

Bhutta, Zulfiqar A., Das, Jai K., Rizvi, Arjumand, Gaffey, Michelle F., Walker, Neff, Horton, Susan, Webb, Patrick, Lartey, Anna, and Black, Robert E. (2013), "Evidence-based interventions for improvement of maternal and child nutrition: What can be done and at what cost?", *The Lancet*, 382(9890), pp. 452–77.

Biber, F. Zümrüt, Unak, Perihan, and Yurt, Fatma (2002), "Stability of iodine content in iodized salt", *Isotopes in Environmental and Health Studies*, 38(2), pp. 87–93.

Black, Maggie, and Fawcett, Ben (2008), *The last taboo: Opening the door on the global sanitation crisis*, Earthscan, London.

Bouis, Howarth E (1999), "Economics of enhanced micronutrient density in food staples", *Field Crops Research*, 60(1–2), pp. 165–73.

——— (2000), "Enrichment of food staples through plant breeding: A new strategy for fighting micronutrient malnutrition", *Nutrition*, 16(7–8), pp. 701–04.

Bressani, Ricardo (2000), "Micronutrient policies for agriculture in Latin America", *Food & Nutrition Bulletin*, 21(4), pp. 538–41.

Bressani, Ricardo, Rooney, Lloyd W., and Salvidar, S.O. (1997), *Fortification of corn masa flour with iron and/or other nutrients: A literature and industry experience review*, SUSTAIN, Washington, DC, URL: pdf.usaid.gov/pdf_docs/pnacc113.pdf.

Bundy, Donald, Burbano, Carmen, Grosh, Margaret, Gelli, Aulo, Jukes, Matthew, and Drake, Lesley (2009), *Rethinking school feeding: Social safety nets, child development and the education*, The World Bank, Washington, DC, URL: openknowledge.worldbank.org/bitstream/handle/10986/2634/48742.pdf.

Cairns, Georgia, Angus, Kathryn, and Hastings, Gerard (2009), *The extent, nature and effects of food promotion to children: A review of the evidence to December 2008*, World Health Organization, Geneva, URL: www.who.int/dietphysicalactivity/publications/marketing_evidence_2009/en/.

Cakmak, Ismail (2008), "Enrichment of cereal grains with zinc: Agronomic or genetic biofortification?", *Plant and Soil*, 302(1–2), pp. 1–17.

——— (2009), "Enrichment of fertilizers with zinc: An excellent investment for humanity and crop production in India", *Journal of Trace Elements in Medicine and Biology*, 23(4), pp. 281–89.

Cakmak, Ismail, Kalaycı, M., Ekiz, H., Braun, H.J., Kılınç, Y., and Yılmaz, A. (1999), "Zinc deficiency as a practical problem in plant and human nutrition in Turkey: A NATO-Science for Stability Project", *Field Crops Research*, 60(1–2), pp. 175–88.

Cao, X.Y., Jiang, X.M., Kareem, A., Dou, Z.H., Abdul Rakeman, M., Zhang, M.L., Ma, T., O'Donnell, K., DeLong, N., and DeLong, G.R. (1994), "Iodination of irrigation water as a method of supplying iodine to a severely iodine-deficient population in Xinjiang, China", *The Lancet*, 344(8915), pp. 107–10.

Carvalho, Susana M.P., and Vasconcelos, Marta W. (2013), "Producing more with less: Strategies and novel technologies for plant-based food biofortification", *Food Research International*, 54(1), pp. 961–71, URL: dx.doi.org/10.1016/j.foodres.2012.12.021.

Cecchini, Simone, and Madariaga, Aldo (2011), *Conditional cash transfer programmes: The recent experience in Latin America and the Caribbean*, Economic Commission for Latin America and the Caribbean, Santiago, Chile, URL: www.cepal.org/en/publications/conditional-cash-transfer-programmes-recent-experience-latin-america-and-caribbean.

Chawla, Dushyant (2014), "Housing conditions in India, 1993–2012", M.Phil. thesis, Jawaharlal Nehru University, New Delhi.

Checchi, Francesco, and Robinson, W. Courtland (2013), *Mortality among populations of southern and central Somalia affected by severe food insecurity and famine during 2010-2012*, Food, Agriculture Organization of United Nations, and Famine Early Warning Systems Network, Rome, URL: www.fsnau.org/downloads/Somalia_Mortality_Estimates_Final_Report_8May2013_upload.pdf.

Coady, David, Grosh, Margaret E., and Hoddinott, John (2004), *Targeting of transfers in developing countries: Review of lessons and experience*, The World Bank, Washington, DC.

Coffey, Diane, Gupta, Aashish, Hathi, Payal, Khurana, Nidhi, Spears, Dean, Srivastav, Nikhil, and Vyas, Sangita (2014), "Revealed preference for open defecation: Evidence from a new survey in rural north India", *Economic and Political Weekly*, 49(38), pp. 43–55.

Cornia, Giovanni Andrea, and Stewart, Frances (1993), "Two errors of targeting", *Journal of International Development*, 5(5), pp. 459–96.

Cunha, Jesse M., De Giorgi, Giacomo, and Jayachandran, Seema (2011), "The price effects of cash versus in-kind transfers", NBER Working Paper No. 17456, National Bureau of Economic Research, Cambridge, MA, URL: www.nber. org/papers/w17456.pdf.

Cunningham, Kenda (2009), "Rural and urban linkages: Operation Flood's role in India's dairy development", IFPRI Discussion Paper 00924, International Food Policy Research Institute, Washington, DC.

Darmon, Nicole, Briend, André, and Drewnowski, Adam (2004), "Energy-dense diets are associated with lower diet costs: A community study of French adults", *Public Health Nutrition*, 7(1), pp. 21–27.

Darmon, Nicole, and Drewnowski, Adam (2008), "Does social class predict diet quality?", *The American Journal of Clinical Nutrition*, 87(5), pp. 1107–17.

Darnton-Hill, Ian, Mora, Jose O., Weinstein, Herbert, Wilbur, Steven, and Nalubola, P. Ritu (1999), "Iron and folate fortification in the Americas to prevent and control micronutrient malnutrition: An analysis", *Nutrition Reviews*, 57(1), pp. 25–31.

Das, S., and Green, A. (2013), "Importance of zinc in crops and human health", *Journal of SAT Agricultural Research*, 11, pp. 1–7.

Dawe, David, Robertson, Richard, and Unnevehr, Laurian (2002), "Golden Rice: What role could it play in alleviation of vitamin A deficiency?", *Food Policy*, 27(5–6), pp. 541–60.

De Benoist, Bruno, Andersson, Maria, Egli, Ines, Takkouche, Bahi, and Allen, Henrietta, eds. (2004), *Iodine status worldwide: WHO global database on iodine deficiency*, World Health Organization, Geneva, URL: whqlibdoc. who.int/publications/2004/9241592001.pdf?ua=1.

De Benoist, Bruno, McLean, Erin, Egli, Ines, and Cogswell, Mary, eds. (2008), *Worldwide prevalence of anaemia, 1993–2005: WHO global database on anaemia*, World Health Organization, Geneva, URL: whqlibdoc.who.int/publications/2008/9789241596657_eng.pdf.

De Schutter, Olivier (2014), *The transformative potential of the right to food*, Report of the Special Rapporteur on the Right to Food, United Nations General Assembly, New York, URL: www . srfood . org / images / stories / pdf / officialreports/20140310_finalreport_en.pdf.

DeClerck, Fabrice A.J., and Negreros-Castillo, Patricia (2000), "Plant species of traditional Mayan homegardens of Mexico as analogs for multistrata agroforests", *Agroforestry Systems*, 48(3), pp. 303–17.

DeLong, G.R., Leslie, P.W., Wang, S.H., Jiang, X.M., Zhang, M.L., Rakeman, M., Jiang, J.Y., Ma, T., and Cao, X.Y. (1997), "Effect on infant mortality of iodination of irrigation water in a severely iodine-deficient area of China", *The Lancet*, 350(9080), pp. 771–73.

DFID (2011), "Scaling up Nutrition: The UK's position paper on undernutrition", Department for International Development, London, URL: www.gov.uk/government/uploads/system/uploads/attachment_data/file/67466/scal-up-nutr-uk-pos-undernutr.pdf.

Diosady, L.L., Alberti, J.O., Mannar, M.G., and FitzgGerald, S. (1998), "Stability of iodine in iodized salt used for correction of iodine-deficiency disorders: II", *Food & Nutrition Bulletin*, 19(3), pp. 240–50.

Drewnowski, Adam (1998), "Energy density, palatability, and satiety: Implications for weight control", *Nutrition Reviews*, 56(12), pp. 347–53.

———— (2010), "The cost of US foods as related to their nutritive value", *The American Journal of Clinical Nutrition*, 92(5), pp. 1181–88.

Drewnowski, Adam, and Darmon, Nicole (2005), "The economics of obesity: Dietary energy density and energy cost", *The American Journal of Clinical Nutrition*, 82(1), 265S–273S.

Drèze, Jean (1990), "Poverty in India and the IRDP delusion", *Economic and Political Weekly*, 25(39), A95–A104.

Drèze, Jean, and Khera, Reetika (2013), "Rural poverty and the public distribution system", *Economic and Political Weekly*, 48(45–46), pp. 55–60.

———— (2015), "Understanding leakages in the public distribution system", *Economic and Political Weekly*, 50(7), pp. 39–42.

Edirisinghe, Neville (1987), *The food stamp scheme in Sri Lanka: Costs, benefits, and options for modification*, International Food Policy Research Institute, Washington, DC, URL: www.ifpri.org/sites/default/files/publications/rr58.pdf.

Ellis, Frank (2012), "We are all poor here: Economic difference, social divisiveness and targeting cash transfers in sub-Saharan Africa", *The Journal of Development Studies*, 48(2), pp. 201–14.

Ellis, Frank, Devereux, Stephen, and White, Philip (2009), *Social protection in Africa*, Edward Elgar Publishing, Cheltenham.

Engel, Susan, and Susilo, Anggun (2014), "Shaming and sanitation in Indonesia: A return to colonial public health practices?", *Development and Change*, 45(1), pp. 157–78, URL: dx.doi.org/10.1111/dech.12075.

Esrey, S.A. (1996), "Water, waste, and well-being: A multicountry study", *American Journal of Epidemiology*, 143(6), pp. 608–23.

Esrey, S.A., Potash, James B., Roberts, Leslie, and Shiff, Clive (1991), "Effects of improved water supply and sanitation on ascariasis, diarrhoea, dracunculiasis, hookworm infection, schistosomiasis, and trachoma", *Bulletin of the World Health Organization*, 69(5), pp. 609–21.

Ezzati, Majid, Lopez, Alan D., Rodgers, Anthony, and Murray, Christopher J.L., eds. (2004), *Comparative quantification of health risks: Global and regional burden of disease attributable to selected major risk factors*, vol. 1, World Health Organization, Geneva.

FAO Global Information and Early Warning System on Food and Agriculture (2010), *Special Alert 329: The Food Situation is of Grave Concern in Parts of the Sahel, Notably in Niger*, GIEWS Special Alert, Food and Agriculture Organization of the United Nations, Rome.

Fernald, Lia C.H. (2013), "Promise, and risks, of conditional cash transfer programmes", *The Lancet*, 382(9886), pp. 7–9.

Fernandes, Erick C.M., and Nair, P.K. Ramachandran (1986), "An evaluation of the structure and function of tropical homegardens", *Agricultural Systems*, 21(4), pp. 279–310.

Food and Agriculture Organization of the United Nations (FAO) (2005), *Voluntary guidelines to support the progressive realization of the right to adequate food in the context of national food security*, Food and Agriculture Organization of the United Nations, Rome, URL: www.fao.org/3/a-y7937e.pdf.

Food and Agriculture Organization of the United Nations (FAO) (2008), *The state of food insecurity in the world, 2008: High food prices and food security – Threats and opportunities*, Food and Agriculture Organization of the United Nations, Rome, URL: www.fao.org/docrep/011/i0291e/i0291e00.htm.

———— (2010), *The state of food insecurity in the world, 2010: Addressing food insecurity in protracted crises*, Food and Agriculture Organization of the United Nations, Rome, URL: www.fao.org/publications/sofi/2014/en/.

———— (2011a), *Global food losses and food waste: Extent, causes and prevention*, Food and Agriculture Organization of the United Nations, Rome, URL: www.fao.org/docrep/014/mb060e/mb060e.pdf.

———— (2011b), *The state of food insecurity in the world, 2011: How does international price volatility affect domestic economies and food security*, Food and Agriculture Organization of the United Nations, Rome, URL: www.fao.org/docrep/014/i2330e/i2330e.pdf.

———— (2012), *The state of food insecurity in the world, 2012: Economic growth is necessary but not sufficient to accelerate reduction of hunger and malnutrition*, Food and Agriculture Organization of the United Nations, Rome, URL: www.fao.org/docrep/016/i3027e/i3027e.pdf.

———— (2013a), *Monitoring and analysing food and agricultural policies in Africa: Synthesis report 2013*, Food and Agriculture Organization of the United Nations, Rome, URL: www.fao.org/3/a-i3513e.pdf.

———— (2013b), *The state of food and agriculture, 2013: Food systems for better nutrition*, Food and Agriculture Organization of the United Nations, Rome, URL: www.fao.org/docrep/018/i3300e/i3300e.pdf.

———— (2014), *Building a common vision for sustainable food and agriculture: Principles and approaches*, Food and Agriculture Organization of the United Nations, Rome.

———— (2015), *The state of food insecurity in the world, 2015: Progress towards the international hunger targets: Final assessment and drivers of change*, Food and Agriculture Organization of the United Nations, Rome.

Garcia, Marito, and Moore, Charity M.T. (2012), *The cash dividend: The rise of cash transfer programs in sub-Saharan Africa*, The World Bank, Washington, DC, URL: ideas.repec.org/b/wbk/wbpubs/2246.html.

Gautam, Dalal, R.S., and Pathak, V. (2010), "Indian dairy sector: Time to revisit Operation Flood", *Livestock Science*, 127(2–3), pp. 164–75.

Ghosh, Jayati (2011), "Cash transfers as the silver bullet for poverty reduction: A sceptical note", *Economic and Political Weekly*, 46(21), pp. 67–71.

———— (2014), "Social protection programmes in India: An overview of recent experiences with different types of schemes", Rome, Food and Agriculture Organization of the United Nations.

Gillespie, Stuart R., McLachlan, Milla, and Shrimpton, Roger, eds. (2003), *Combating malnutrition: Time to act*, Health, Nutrition, and Population (HNP) Series, The World Bank, Washington, DC.

Grisa, Catia, and Schmitt, Claudia Job (2013), "The Food Acquisition Programme in Brazil: Contributions to biodiversity, food security and nutrition", in Fanzo, Jessica, Hunter, Danny, Borelli, Teresa, and Mattei, Federico, eds., *Diversifying food and diets: Using agricultural biodiversity to improve nutrition and health*, Routledge, London and New York.

Grusak, Michael A. (2005), "Golden Rice gets a boost from maize", *Nature Biotechnology*, 23(4), pp. 429–30.

Guhan, S. (1980), "Rural poverty policy and play acting", *Economic and Political Weekly*, 15(47), pp. 1975–82.

Haider, Batool A., and Bhutta, Zulfiqar A. (2015), "Neonatal vitamin A supplementation: Time to move on", *The Lancet*, 385(9975), pp. 1268–71.

Hanchett, Suzanne, Krieger, Laurie, Kahn, Mohidul Hoque, Kullmann, Craig, and Ahmed, Rokeya (2011), *Long-term sustainability of improved sanitation in rural Bangladesh*, The World Bank, Washington, DC.

HarvestPlus (2014), *Biofortification progress briefs*, HarvestPlus, Washington, DC, URL: www.harvestplus.org/sites/default/files/Biofortification_Progress_Briefs_August2014_WEB_0.pdf.

Hastings, Gerard, McDermott, Laura, Angus, Kathryn, Stead, Martine, and Thomson, Stephen (2006), *The extent, nature and effects of food promotion to children: A review of the evidence*, World Health Organization, Geneva, URL: www.who.int/dietphysicalactivity/publications/Hastings_paper_marketing.pdf.

Herforth, Anna, and Hoberg, Yurie Tanimichi (2014), *Learning from World Bank history: Agriculture and food-based approaches for addressing malnutrition*, Agriculture and Environmental Services Discussion Paper No 10, The World Bank, Washington, DC.

Hertrampf, Eva (2002), "Iron fortification in the Americas", *Nutrition Reviews*, 60, pp. S22–S25.

Hidrobo, Melissa, Hoddinott, John, Peterman, Amber, Margolies, Amy, and Moreira, Vanessa (2014), "Cash, food, or vouchers? Evidence from a randomized experiment in northern Ecuador", *Journal of Development Economics*, 107, pp. 144–56.

High Level Panel of Experts (HLPE) (2011), *Price volatility and food security: A report by the High Level Panel of Experts on food security and nutrition*, Committee on World Food Security, Rome, URL: www.fao.org/3/a-mb737e.pdf.

Himanshu, and Sen, Abhijit (2013), "In-kind food transfers–I", *Economic and Political Weekly*, 48(45–46), pp. 46–58.

Hoddinott, John, Sandström, Susanna, and Upton, Joanna (2013), *Impact evaluation of cash and food transfers in Zinder, Niger: Analytical report*, World Food Programme, Rome, URL: documents.wfp.org/stellent/groups/public/documents/resources/wfp257676.%20pdf.

Holzmann, Robert, Sherburne-Benz, Lynne, and Tesliuc, Emil (2003), *Social risk management: The World Bank's approach to social protection in a globalizing world*, Social Protection Department, The World Bank, Washington, DC, URL: siteresources.worldbank.org/SOCIALPROTECTION/Publications/20847129/SRMWBApproachtoSP.pdf.

Horton, Richard (2014), "Offline: Why the sustainable development goals will fail", *The Lancet*, 383(9936), p. 2196.

Horton, Susan (2008), "The economics of nutritional interventions", in Semba, Richard D., and Bloem, Martin W., eds., *Nutrition and health in developing countries (second edition)*, Humana Press, New Jersey.

Horton, Susan, and Ross, Jay (2003), "The economics of iron deficiency", *Food Policy*, 28(1), pp. 51–75.

Hotz, Christine, Loechl, Cornelia, Brauw, Alan de, Eozenou, Patrick, Gilligan, Daniel, Moursi, Mourad, Munhaua, Bernardino, Jaarsveld, Paul van, Carriquiry, Alicia, and Meenakshi, J.V. (2012a), "A large-scale intervention to introduce orange sweet potato in rural Mozambique increases vitamin A intakes among children and women", *British Journal of Nutrition*, 108(1), pp. 163–76.

Hotz, Christine, Loechl, Cornelia, Lubowa, Abdelrahman, Tumwine, James K., Ndeezi, Grace, Nandutu Masawi, Agnes, Baingana, Rhona, Carriquiry, Alicia, Brauw, Alan de, Meenakshi, Jonnalagadda V., and Gilligan, Daniel O. (2012b), "Introduction of β-Carotene-Rich orange sweet potato in rural Uganda results in increased vitamin A intakes among children and women and improved vitamin A status among children", *The Journal of Nutrition*, 142(10), pp. 1871–80.

Hueso, Andres, and Bell, Brian (2013), "An untold story of policy failure: The Total Sanitation Campaign in India", *Water Policy*, 15(6), pp. 1001–17.

International Food Policy Research Institute (IFPRI) (2014), *Global nutrition report: Actions and accountability to accelerate the world's progress on nutrition*, International Food Policy Research Institute, Washington, DC, URL: www.ifpri.org/sites/default/files/publications/gnr14.pdf.

International Labour Office (ILO) (2008), *Can low-income countries afford basic social security?*, International Labour Office, Geneva, URL: www.ilo.org/wcmsp5/groups/public/---asia/---ro-bangkok/---ilo-manila/documents/publication/wcms_126217.pdf.

———— (2012), *Social protection floor for a fair and inclusive globalization: Report of the advisory group chaired by Michelle Bachelet convened by the ILO with the collaboration of the WHO*, International Labour Office, Geneva, URL: www.ilo.org/public/english/protection/spfag/download/background/bachrep_en.pdf.

Jacob, J. (1997), "Structure analysis and system dynamics of agroforestry homegardens of southern Kerala", PhD thesis, Department of Agronomy, College of Agriculture, Kerala Agricultural University, Thiruvananthapuram.

———— (2014), "Homestead farming in Kerala: A multi-faceted land-use system", *Review of Agrarian Studies*, 4(1), pp. 80–94.

Jha, L.K., Rau, S.K., Bhatti, I.Z., Dastur, N.N., Bhattacharya, P., and Shirali, A.R. (1984), "Report of the Evaluation Committee on Operation Flood II", Department of Agriculture and Cooperation, Ministry of Agriculture, Government of India, New Delhi.

Jones, Nicholas R.V., Conklin, Annalijn I., Suhrcke, Marc, and Monsivais, Pablo (2014), "The growing price gap between more and less healthy foods: Analysis of a novel longitudinal UK dataset", *PLoS ONE*, 9(10).

Jooste, Pieter L., Weight, Michael J., and Lombard, Carl J. (2000), "Short-term effectiveness of mandatory iodization of table salt, at an elevated iodine concentration, on the iodine and goiter status of schoolchildren with endemic goiter", *The American Journal of Clinical Nutrition*, 71(1), pp. 75–80.

Josling, Tim (2011), "Global food stamps: An idea worth considering?", International Centre for Trade and Sustainable Development, Geneva.

Kakwani, Nanak, Soares, Fábio Veras, and Son, Hyun H. (2005), "Conditional cash transfers in African countries", Working Paper 9, International Policy Centre for Inclusive Growth, Brasilia, URL: ideas.repec.org/p/ipc/wpaper/9.html.

Kar, Kamal, and Chambers, Robert (2008), *Handbook on Community-led Total Sanitation*, Plan UK and Institute of Development Studies, London and Sussex, URL: www.communityledtotalsanitation.org/sites/communityledtotalsanitation.org/files/cltshandbook.pdf.

Kar, Kamal, and Pasteur, Katherine (2005), "Subsidy or self-respect?: Community Led Total Sanitation: An update on recent developments", IDS Working Paper 257, Institute of Development Studies, Sussex, URL: www.ids.ac.uk/files/wp257.pdf.

Kelly, F.C. (1953), "Studies on the Stability of Iodine Compounds in Iodized Salt", *Bulletin of the World Health Organization*, 9(2), pp. 217–30.

Khera, Reetika (2011a), "Revival of the public distribution system: Evidence and explanations", *Economic and Political Weekly*, 46(44–45), pp. 36–50.

——— (2011b), "Trends in diversion of grain from the public distribution system", *Economic and Political Weekly*, 46(21), pp. 106–14.

Krishnamurthy, Prasad, Pathania, Vikram, and Tandon, Sharad (2014), "The impacts of reforms to the public distribution system in India's Chhattisgarh on food security", Economic Research Report Number 164, Economic Research Service, United States Department of Agriculture, Washington DC, URL: www.ers.usda.gov/media/1332421/err164.pdf.

Kulkarni, Seema, O'Reilly, Kathleen, and Bhat, Sneha (2014), "Sanitation vulnerability: Women's stress and struggles for violence–free sanitation", Pune, Society for Promoting Participative Eco-system Management.

Kumar, Anjani, Joshi, P.K., Kumar, Praduman, and Parappurathu, Shinoj (2014), "Trends in the consumption of milk and milk products in India: Implications for self-sufficiency in milk production", *Food Security*, 6(5), pp. 719–26, URL: dx.doi.org/10.1007/s12571-014-0376-y.

Kumar, Arjun (2015), "Discrepancies in sanitation statistics of rural India", *Economic and Political Weekly*, 50(2), pp. 13–15, URL: www.epw.in/commentary/discrepancies-sanitation-statistics-rural-india.html.

Kurien, Verghese (2004), "India's milk revolution: Investing in rural producer organizations", paper presented at the Conference on Scaling Up Poverty Reduction: A Global Learning, Shanghai, The World Bank, Washington DC, URL: www-wds.worldbank.org/external/default/WDSContentServer/WDSP/IB/2004/12/08/000090341_20041208112649/Rendered/PDF/308270IN0Milk01ion01see0also0307591.pdf.

Layrisse, Miguel, Martinez-Torres, Carlos, Renzi, Marta, Velez, Fermin, and González, Magdalena (1976), "Sugar as a vehicle for iron fortification", *The American Journal of Clinical Nutrition*, 29(1), pp. 8–18, URL: ajcn.nutrition.org/content/29/1/8.abstract.

Lokshin, Michael, Das Gupta, Monica, Gragnolati, Michele, and Ivaschenko, Oleksiy (2005), "Improving child nutrition? the integrated child development services in India", *Development and Change*, 36(4), pp. 613–40, URL: dx.doi.org/10.1111/j.0012-155X.2005.00427.x.

Longhurst, Richard (2010), "Global leadership for nutrition: The UN's Standing Committee on Nutrition (SCN) and its contributions", IDS Discussion Paper 390, Institute of Development Studies, Sussex.

Manley, James, Gitter, Seth, and Slavchevska, Vanya (2013), "How effective are cash transfers at improving nutritional status?", *World Development*, 48, pp. 133–55.

Mann, Neelakshi, and Pande, Varad (2012), *MGNREGA sameeksha: An anthology of research studies on the Mahatma Gandhi National Rural Employment Guarantee Act 2005, 2006–2012*, Ministry of Rural Development (MoRD), Government of India and Orient Blackswan, Hyderabad.

Mason, John, Greiner, Ted, Shrimpton, Roger, Sanders, David, and Yukich, Joshua (2015), "Vitamin A policies need rethinking", *International Journal of Epidemiology*, 44(1), pp. 283–92.

Mayer, Jorge E., Pfeiffer, Wolfgang H., and Beyer, Peter (2008), "Biofortified crops to alleviate micronutrient malnutrition", *Current Opinion in Plant Biology*, 11(2), pp. 166–70.

Mayes, S., Massawe, F.J., Alderson, P.G., Roberts, J.A., Azam-Ali, S.N., and Hermann, M. (2011), "The potential for underutilized crops to improve security of food production", *Journal of Experimental Botany*, 63(3), pp. 1075–79.

McKeon, Nora (2014), *Food security governance: Empowering communities, regulating corporations*, Routledge, London.

Meenakshi, J.V., Johnson, Nancy L., Manyong, Victor M., DeGroote, Hugo, Javelosa, Josyline, Yanggen, David R., Naher, Firdousi, Gonzalez, Carolina, García, James, and Meng, Erika (2010), "How cost-effective is biofortification in combating micronutrient malnutrition? An ex ante assessment", *World Development*, 38(1), pp. 64–75.

Méndez, V. Ernesto, Lok, Rosana, and Somarriba, Edwardo (2001), "Interdisciplinary analysis of homegardens in Nicaragua: Micro-zonation, plant use and socioeconomic importance", *Agroforestry Systems*, 51(2), pp. 85–96.

Mkandawire, Thandika (2005), "Targeting and universalism in poverty reduction", Social Policy and Development Programme Paper Number 23, United Nations Research Institute for Social Development, Geneva.

Mokoro (2015), *Independent comprehensive evaluation of the Scaling Up Nutrition movement*, Mokoro Ltd, Oxford, URL: scalingupnutrition.org/wp-content/uploads/2015/05/SUN_ICE_FullReport-All(1-5-15).pdf.

Moodie, Rob, Stuckler, David, Monteiro, Carlos, Sheron, Nick, Neal, Bruce, Thamarangsi, Thaksaphon, Lincoln, Paul, and Casswell, Sally (2013), "Profits and pandemics: Prevention of harmful effects of tobacco, alcohol, and ultra-processed food and drink industries", *The Lancet*, 381(9867), pp. 670–79.

Morris, Saul S., Cogill, Bruce, and Uauy, Ricardo (2008), "Effective international action against undernutrition: Why has it proven so difficult and what can be done to accelerate progress?", *The Lancet*, 371(9612), pp. 608–21.

Natalicchio, Marcela, Garrett, James, Mulder-Sibanda, Menno, Ndegwa, Steve, and Voorbraak, Doris, eds. (2009), *Carrots and sticks: The political economy of nutrition policy reforms*, HNP Discussion Paper No 10, The World Bank, Washington, DC.

National Sample Survey Organization (NSSO) (2014), *Level and pattern of consumer expenditure, 2011–12*, NSS 68th Round, July 2011-June 2012, Report

No. 555, New Delhi, National Sample Survey Organization, Ministry of Statistics and Programme Implementation, Government of India.

National University of Educational Planning and Administratio (NUEPA) (2014), *School education in India*, National University of Educational Planning and Administration, New Delhi.

Nishida, Chizuru (2013), "Nutrition policies: From 1992 ICN to 2014 ICN2", Preparatory Technical Meeting, Second International Conference on Nutrition (ICN2), 13–15 November, Food and Agriculture Organization of the United Nations (FAO), Rome, URL: www.slideshare.net/FAOoftheUN/nutrition-policiesfrom-1992-icn-to-2014-icn2.

Okafor, J.C., and Fernandes, E.C.M. (1987), "Compound farms of southeastern Nigeria", *Agroforestry Systems*, 5(2), pp. 153–68.

Padoch, Christine, and De Jong, Wil (1991), "The house gardens of Santa Rosa: Diversity and variability in an Amazonian agricultural system", *Economic Botany*, 45(2), pp. 166–75.

Pangaribowo, Evita Hanie (2012), "Food security program in the time of economic crisis: A lesson to learn from Indonesia", 52nd Annual Conference, 26–28 September, German Association of Agricultural Economists (GEWISOLA), Stuttgart.

Peraci, Adoniram Sanches, and Bittencourt, Gilson Alceu (2011), "Family farming and price guarantee programs in Brazil: The food procurement program (PAA)", in Silva, José Graziano da, Del Grossi, Mauro Eduardo, França, Caio Galvão de, and Vasconcelos, Luiz Marcos, eds., *The Fome Zero (Zero Hunger) Program: the Brazilian experience*, Ministry of Agrarian Development, Brazil.

Pineda, Oscar (1998), "Fortification of sugar with vitamin A", *Food and Nutrition Bulletin*, 19(2), pp. 131–36, URL: www.ingentaconnect.com/content/nsinf/fnb/1998/00000019/00000002/art00007.

Pinstrup-Andersen, Per (2013), "Nutrition-sensitive food systems: From rhetoric to action", *The Lancet*, 382(9890), pp. 375–76.

Pruss-Ustun, Annette, Kay, David, Fewtrell, Lorna, and Bartram, Jamie (2004), "Unsafe water, sanitation and hygiene", in Ezzati, Majid, Lopez, Alan D., Rodgers, Anthony, and Murray, Christopher J.L., eds., *Comparative quantification of health risks: Global and regional burden of disease attributable to selected major risk factors*, vol. 2, World Health Organization, Geneva.

Rasheed, Sabrina, Hanifi, Manzoor A., Iqbal, Md, Nazma, Nandita, and Bhuiya, Abbas (2001), "Policy of universal salt iodization in Bangladesh: Do coastal people benefit?", *Journal of Health, Population and Nutrition*, 19(2), pp. 66–72.

Rath, Nilakantha (1985), "Garibi hatao: Can IRDP do it?", *Economic and Political Weekly*, 20(6), pp. 238–46.

Rawal, Vikas, and Saha, Partha (2015), "Women's employment in India: What do recent NSS surveys of employment and unemployment show?", *Statistics on Indian Economy and Society*, URL: indianstatistics.org/2015/01/28/women-workers.html.

Reich, Michael R., and Balarajan, Yarlini (2012), *Political economy analysis for food and nutrition security*, The World Bank, Washington, DC.

Rengel, Z., Batten, G.D., and Crowley, D.E. (1999), "Agronomic approaches for improving the micronutrient density in edible portions of field crops", *Field Crops Research*, 60(1–2), pp. 27–40.

Renner, Rebecca (2010), "Dietary iodine: Why are so many mothers not getting enough?", *Environmental Health Perspectives*, 118(10), pp. A438–A442.

Richter, Judith (2015), "Conflicts of interest and global health and nutrition governance: The illusion of robust principles", *The British Medical Journal*, URL: www.bmj.com/content/349/bmj.g5457/rr.

Robinson, Andy (2005), *Scaling-up rural sanitation in South Asia: Lessons learned from Bangladesh, India, and Pakistan*, Water and Sanitation Program-South Asia, The World Bank, New Delhi, URL: esa.un.org/iys/docs/san_lib_docs/ Scaling%20Up%20Rural%20Saniltation.pdf.

Rowe, Sylvia, Alexander, Nick, Clydesdale, Fergus M., Applebaum, Rhona S., Atkinson, Stephanie, Black, Richard M., Dwyer, Johanna T., Hentges, Eric, Higley, Nancy A., Lefevre, Michael, Lupton, Joanne R., Miller, Sanford A., Tancredi, Doris L., Weaver, Connie M., Woteki, Catherine E., and Wedral, Elaine (2009), "Funding food science and nutrition research: Financial conflicts and scientific integrity", *The American Journal of Clinical Nutrition*, pp. 1285–91.

Sabates-Wheeler, Rachel, and Devereux, Stephen (2010), "Cash transfers and high food prices: Explaining outcomes on Ethiopia's productive safety net programme", *Food Policy*, 35(4), pp. 274–85.

Saltzman, Amy, Birol, Ekin, Bouis, Howarth E., Boy, Erick, Moura, Fabiana F. De, Islam, Yassir, and Pfeiffer, Wolfgang H. (2013), "Biofortification: Progress toward a more nourishing future", *Global Food Security*, 2(1), pp. 9–17.

Sanan, Deepak, and Moulik, Soma Ghosh (2007), *Community-led Total Sanitation in rural areas: An approach that works*, Water and Sanitation Program-South Asia, The World Bank, New Delhi, URL: esa.un.org/iys/docs/san_ lib_docs/WSP-Community%20Led.pdf.

Scaling Up Nutrition (SUN) (2009), *Scaling up nutrition: A framework for action*, Scaling Up Nutrition, Geneva, URL: scalingupnutrition.org/wp-content/ uploads/pdf/SUN_Framework.pdf.

Sen, Amartya (1995), "The political economy of targeting", in Van de Walle, Dominique, and Nead, Kimberly, eds., *Public spending and the poor: Theory and evidence*, The Johns Hopkins University Press, Baltimore and London.

Shankar, Kripa (1991), "Integrated Rural Development Programme in Eastern UP", *Economic and Political Weekly*, 26(41), pp. 2339–40.

Shankar, Shylashri, and Gaiha, Raghav (2013), *Battling corruption: Has NREGA reached India's rural poor?*, Oxford University Press, New Delhi.

Sharma, Aarushie, Aasaavari, Asmita, and Anand, Srishty (2015), "Understanding issues involved in toilet access for women", *Economic and Political Weekly*, 50(34), pp. 70–74, URL: www.epw.in/notes/understanding-issues-involved-toilet-access-women.html.

Sidaner, Emilie, Balaban, Daniel, and Burlandy, Luciene (2013), "The Brazilian school feeding programme: An example of an integrated programme in support of food and nutrition security", *Public Health Nutrition*, 16(06), pp. 989–94.

Silva, José Graziano da, Del Grossi, Mauro Eduardo, França, Caio Galvão de, and Vasconcelos, Luiz Marcos, eds. (2011), *The Fome Zero (Zero Hunger)*

Program: The Brazilian experience, Ministry of Agrarian Development, Brasilia.

Singh, Shamsher (2014), "Access to basic amenities: A sociological study of villages in selected states of India", PhD thesis, Department of Sociology, University of Calcutta, Kolkata.

Sinha, Dipa (2013), "Cost of implementing the National Food Security Act", *Economic and Political Weekly*, 48(39), pp. 31–4.

Smith, Lisa C., and Haddad, Lawrence (2015), "Reducing child undernutrition: Past drivers and priorities for the post-MDG era", *World Development*, 68, pp. 180–204.

Smith, Pete (2013), "Delivering food security without increasing pressure on land", *Global Food Security*, 2(1), pp. 18–23.

Soares, Fábio Veras, Nehring, Ryan, Schwengber, Rovane Battaglin, Rodrigues, Clarissa Guimarães, Lambais, Guilherme, Balaban, Daniel Silva, Jones, Cynthia, and Galante, Andrea (2013), *Structured demand and smallholder farmers in Brazil: The case of PAA and PNAE*, International Policy Centre for Inclusive Growth, Brasilia-DF, URL: www . ipc - undp . org / pub / IPCTechnicalPaper7.pdf.

Spears, Dean (2013), *How much international variation in child height can sanitation explain?*, The World Bank, Washington, DC, URL: openknowledge.worldb ank.com/handle/10986/13163.

Speeckaert, Marijn M., Speeckaert, Reinhart, Wierckx, Katrien, Delanghe, Joris R., and Kaufman, Jean-Marc (2011), "Value and pitfalls in iodine fortification and supplementation in the 21st century", *British Journal of Nutrition*, 106(7), pp. 964–73.

Statistics South Africa (2012), *Income and expenditure of households, 2010/2011*, Statistical Release, Statistics South Africa, Pretoria, URL: microdata . worl dbank.org/index.php/catalog/1545/download/25340.

Stein, Alexander J., Meenakshi, J.V., Qaim, Matin, Nestel, Penelope, Sachdev, H.P.S., and Bhutta, Zulfiqar A. (2008), "Potential impacts of iron biofortification in India", *Social Science & Medicine*, 66(8), pp. 1797–808.

Stein, Alexander J., Sachdev, H.P.S., and Qaim, Matin (2008), "Genetic engineering for the poor: Golden Rice and public health in India", *World Development*, 36(1), pp. 144–58, URL: www . sciencedirect . com / science / article / pii / S0305750X0700191X.

Sumarto, Sudarno, Suryahadi, Asep, and Widyanti, Wenefrida (2005), "Assessing the impact of Indonesian social safety net programmes on household welfare and poverty dynamics", *The European Journal of Development Research*, 17(1), pp. 155–77.

Sunwar, Sharmila, Thornström, Carl-Gustaf, Subedi, Anil, and Bystrom, Marie (2006), "Home gardens in western Nepal: Opportunities and challenges for on-farm management of agrobiodiversity", *Biodiversity and Conservation*, 15(13), pp. 4211–38.

Swaminathan, Madhura (2000), *Weakening welfare: The public distribution of food in India*, LeftWord Books, New Delhi.

——— (2004), "Targeted food stamps", *The Hindu*, 3 August, URL: www.thehindu. com/2004/08/03/stories/2004080300331000.htm.

Swaminathan, Madhura, and Misra, Neeta (2001), "Errors of targeting: Public distribution of food in a Maharashtra village, 1995-2000", *Economic and Political Weekly*, 36(26), pp. 2447–54.

Swaminathan, Madhura, and Singh, Shamsher (2014), "Exclusion in access to basic civic amenities: Evidence from fourteen villages", in Ramachandran, V.K., and Swaminathan, Madhura, eds., *Dalit Households in Village Economies*, Tulika Books, New Delhi.

Swensson, Luana F. Joppert (2015), *Institutional procurement of food from small-holder farmers*, Food and Agriculture Organization of the United Nations, Rome, URL: www.fao.org/fileadmin/user_upload/ivc/PDF/Institutional_Procurement_of_Food_from_Smallholder_Farmers_Brazil.pdf.

Tabor, Steven R., and Sawit, M. Husein (2001), "Social protection via rice: The OPK rice subsidy program in Indonesia", *The Developing Economies*, 39(3), pp. 267–94.

Talukder, A., Haselow, N.J., Osei, A.K., Villate, E., Reario, D., Kroeun, H., SokHoing, L., Uddin, A., Dhunge, S., and Quinn, V. (2010), "Homestead food production model contributes to improved household food security and nutrition status of young children and women in poor populations: Lessons learned from scaling-up programs in Asia (Bangladesh, Cambodia, Nepal and Philippines)", *Field Actions Science Reports, The Journal of Field Actions*, (Special Issue 1), pp. 1–9.

Temple, Norman J., and Steyn, Nelia P. (2009), "Food prices and energy density as barriers to healthy food patterns in Cape Town, South Africa", *Journal of Hunger & Environmental Nutrition*, 4(2), pp. 203–13.

———— (2011), "The cost of a healthy diet: A South African perspective", *Nutrition*, 27(5), pp. 505–08.

Temple, Norman J., Steyn, Nelia P., Fourie, Jean, and De Villiers, Anniza (2011), "Price and availability of healthy food: A study in rural South Africa", *Nutrition*, 27(1), pp. 55–58.

Thorat, Sukhadeo (2009), *Dalits in India: Search for a common destiny*, Sage Publications, New Delhi.

UNICEF (1990), *Strategy for improved nutrition of children and women in developing countries*, UNICEF, New York, URL: www.ceecis.org/iodine/01_global/01_pl/01_01_other_1992_unicef.pdf.

———— (2008), *The state of the world's children, 2009: Maternal and newborn health*, UNICEF, New York.

———— (2013), *Improving child nutrition: The achievable imperative for global progress*, UNICEF, New York.

United Nations (2012), "UN Secretary-General appoints 27 global leaders to head worldwide effort to address child malnutrition", April, United Nations Press Release, URL: scalingup.staging.wpengine.com/wp-content/uploads/2012/09/120410-SUN-Lead-Group-release-SG-Appoints-27-leaders-to-head-SUN.pdf.

United Nations Economic and Social Council (1976), "Food problems: Institutional arrangements relating to nutrition", Sixty-first session, E/5805, 28 April, United Nations Economic and Social Council, URL: http://www.unscn.org/files/mandate/ECOSOC_statement__re_SCN_E5805_April_1976.pdf.

———— (1977), "Institutional arrangements relating to nutrition: Supplementary statement by the Administrative Committee on Co-ordination", Sixty-third session, E/5968, 26 April, United Nations Economic and Social Council, URL: http://www.unscn.org/files/mandate/ECOSOC_suppl_statement_ on_establishment_of_SCN_April_1977.pdf.

USAID (2014), *Multi-sectoral nutrition strategy, 2014-2025,* US Agency for International Development, Washington, DC, URL: www.usaid.gov/sites/default/ files/documents/1867/USAID_Nutrition_Strategy_5-09_508.pdf.

Usami, Yoshifumi, and Rawal, Vikas (2012), "Some aspects of the implementation of India's employment guarantee", *Review of Agrarian Studies,* 2(2), pp. 74–105.

Varo, Pertti, Alfthan, G., Ekholm, P., Aro, A., and Koivistoinen, P. (1988), "Selenium intake and serum selenium in Finland: Effects of soil fertilization with selenium", *The American Journal of Clinical Nutrition,* 48(2), pp. 324–29, URL: ajcn.nutrition.org/content/48/2/324.abstract.

Wang, Dong D., Leung, Cindy W., Li, Yanping, Ding, Eric L., Chiuve, Stephanie E., Hu, Frank B., and Willett, Walter C. (2014), "Trends in dietary quality among adults in the United States: 1999 through 2010", *JAMA Internal Medicine,* 174(10), pp. 1587–95.

Weiss, John (2005), *Poverty targeting in Asia,* Edward Elgar Publishing, Cheltenham.

Wojcicki, Janet M., and Heyman, Melvin B. (2010), "Malnutrition and the role of the soft drink industry in improving child health in sub-Saharan Africa", *Pediatrics,* 126(6), pp. 1617–21.

World Bank (2006), *Repositioning nutrition as central to development: A strategy for large-scale action,* The World Bank, Washington, DC, URL: siteresources. worldbank.org/nutrition/Resources/281846-1131636806329/NutritionStr ategy.pdf.

——— (2015), *World Development Report, 2015: Mind, society and behavior,* The World Bank, Washington, DC.

World Food Programme (2013), *State of school feeding worldwide, 2013,* World Food Programme, Rome.

World Health Organization (WHO) (2008), *Salt as a vehicle for fortification: Report of a WHO expert consultation,* World Health Organization, Geneva, URL: apps.who.int/iris/bitstream/10665/43908/1/9789241596787_eng.pdf?ua= 1.

——— (2009), *Global prevalence of vitamin A deficiency in populations at risk, 1995–2005: WHO global database on vitamin A deficiency,* World Health Organization, Geneva.

——— (2012), *Guideline: Sodium intake for adults and children,* World Health Organization, Geneva, URL: www . who . int / nutrition / publications / guidelines/sodium_intake_printversion.pdf.

——— (2013), *Essential nutrition actions: Improving maternal, newborn, infant and young child health and nutrition,* World Health Organization, Geneva, URL: apps.who.int/iris/bitstream/10665/84409/1/9789241505550_eng.pdf?ua= 1.

——— (2015), *Using price policies to promote healthier diets,* Regional Office for Europe, World Health Organization, Copenhagen.

World Health Organization (WHO), and Food and Agriculture Organization of the United Nations (FAO) (2003), *Diet, nutrition and the prevention of chronic diseases,* Report of a Joint WHO/FAO Expert Consultation. WHO

Technical Report Series 916, World Health Organization, Geneva, URL: whqlibdoc.who.int/trs/who_trs_916.pdf.

Zimmermann, Michael B., Aeberli, Isabelle, Torresani, Toni, and Burgi, Hans (2005), "Increasing the iodine concentration in the Swiss iodized salt program markedly improved iodine status in pregnant women and children: A 5-y prospective national study", *The American Journal of Clinical Nutrition*, 82(2), pp. 388–92.

Index